# THE ART OF THE AUTHOR INTERVIEW

# The Art of the AUTHOR INTERVIEW

## And Interviewing Creative People

## Sarah Anne Johnson

UNIVERSITY PRESS OF NEW ENGLAND

HANOVER AND LONDON

Published by University Press of New England,
One Court Street, Lebanon, NH 03766
www.upne.com
© 2005 by Sarah Anne Johnson
Printed in the United States of America
5  4  3  2  1

Library of Congress Cataloging-in-Publication Data

Johnson, Sarah Anne.
The art of the author interview : and interviewing creative people / Sarah Anne Johnson.
  p.  cm.
ISBN 1–58465–397–3 (pbk. : alk. paper)
  1. Interviews—Authorship. 2. Authors—Interviews—Methodology. 3. Interviewing. I. Title.
PN171.166J65 2005                                    2004023688

*For my Alice*

# Contents

# Acknowledgments

I'd like to thank the many editors, publications, and permissions people who generously answered questions and provided quotes and permissions for this book, including *BOMB, The Brooklyn Rail, The Cape Cod Voice, Michigan Quarterly Review, Missouri Review, Paris Review, Poets & Writers, The Writer,* and *The Writer's Chronicle,* also *Fresh Air with Terry Gross.* I'd also like to thank the talented people at the University Press of New England who worked hard to bring this book to life, especially my editor John W. Landrigan. Thanks also to my family who come to every event; to Amy Yelin and Ellen Santasiero for donating samples of their work; to Liam Rector, Steven Cramer, David Fenza for providing forums in which "The Art of the Author Interview" can be discussed and explored. Thank you to Jason Shinder who taught me how to make books happen. And thanks to the Posse for helping me hold my course; to Miriam for staying in the boat with me even through the storms; and to Susan, my constant creative consort, my muse and companion on this wild, tempestuous sea.

# Introduction

An interview is a performance, and although a performance can reveal much, its revelations are selective, and its omissions and concealments are often as instructive as its grand pronouncements. Sometimes a writer doesn't want to tell; sometimes a writer doesn't know; sometimes a writer has forgotten. But why should a writer tell all? Why should anyone? In the interview, we must largely settle for conversation instead.

—Margaret Atwood, *Women Writers at Work*

In its simplest terms, an interview is a conversation between two people, and like any conversation, questions are asked and truths revealed. The most satisfying conversations are those in which we learn something we didn't expect to learn, or identify in some particular way with the person we're talking to, or articulate something we hadn't previously stated. I'm thinking of a conversation I had recently with Chitra Banerjee Divakaruni, in which she was talking about writing *The Vine of Desire*. She realized partway through that the book was a meditation on desire, and she then was able to add vignettes or single-line images that resonated with that theme, like ripples around a rock tossed in the water.

The difference between an author interview and an ordinary conversation is that the author interview has an *explicit purpose*. That purpose is in the mind of the interviewer from the outset of the conversation. Whether it's to explore the author's body of work, or discuss the writing life and the creative process, or perhaps to discuss a favorite novel, the purpose will shape the conversation to follow. And beneath that explicit purpose is the less direct intention of the interviewer simply to *reveal the writer*. Authors often remain aloof, content to live within the confines of their creations and to make only the rare public appearances necessary to promote their work. We don't have constant access to the lives of our favorite writers. There is no *People* magazine equivalent for writers, no *National Enquirer* displaying cover photos of Ann Patchett walking her dog

*Epigraph*: Margaret Atwood, introduction to *Women Writers at Work*, edited by George Plimpton (New York: Penguin Books, 1989).

with Elizabeth McCracken, no headlines blasting "Well-Known Novelists Seen Discussing New Works in Public! Exclusive Photos!"

And yet there is a real need in our culture to hear the voices of artists, those who seek to reveal the deeper meanings in our lives. The popularity of book discussion groups and online forums demonstrates this national interest in reading and understanding literature in new and meaningful ways, as does the expansive enrollment in writing programs across the country. Even television talk shows with on-air book clubs host author interviews, all in an effort to meet this need in our society to hear from writers and other artists. Historically, writers and artists are on the leading edge of ideas. They are spokespeople for our cultural and personal experiences, as they provide the lenses through which we view the world and our own experiences.

People are more interested than ever in hearing from the writers of the books they love. In the same way that it's not enough just to see a movie—we want to read about how it was made, and watch the DVD features, and read about the actors in *People,* or better yet, hear them interviewed on *In the Actor's Studio*—it's no longer enough to read the book. We want to talk about it. We want to hear the author talk about it, as if through asking and probing we might finally discover the secret source of the writer's magic, the elements of creation that bore a fictive world so authentically into our imaginations. We want to understand the person who created the characters we've come to love or hate or, more importantly, understand. We know them, and we hope through conversation with the author to be reintroduced to them in the living flesh. We want our character friends back, and we hope that hearing the author's voice will ease our longing for the story that took up an hour, a day, a week, a month of our lives.

In addition to being simply a conversation, the author interview is a literary document that takes as its seed the transcript of that conversation between author and interviewer, through revision and contemplation, this transcript becomes a piece of literature. The interview, if published, becomes part of the literary canon, part of the archive of writings on the particular author interviewed and, more importantly, part of the national literary dialogue about literature, writing, creativity, and any number of other subjects broached in the discussion. A published author interview will be a reference for any journalist, scholar, writer, or reader interested in knowing about the author.

The author interview is also a tool for promoting the author's work. Often authors are more likely to agree to interviews when they have a new book to promote in the media. These interviews are then included in the press kits that a publisher distributes to the media, bookstores, and other promotional outlets. The need for promoting one's work, even when a new book is not in the offing, often drives authors to take time away from their writing for an interview.

The interview is also a promotional tool for the interviewer. When the interview is published, the interviewer gets a biographical note in the publication and can list her publications, promote her work, and thereby gain some name recognition. Many writers find agents for their own work through the exposure they receive by publishing literary criticism such as book reviews, author interviews, or articles about writing. People in the publishing industry are always on the lookout for real talent. When an agent notices in the biographical note that the creator of the wonderful author interview he just read is working on a novel, he wants to find out more.

## Building a Literary Life

Any creative person pursuing an art needs to build a life that supports and sustains that work. Many creative people choose to attend graduate or other types of programs, in which they receive the support and stimulation they need to further develop their work, while others go it alone. In either case, building an artistic life, or in the case of the writer, a literary life, is critical. But let's take a moment to think about what constitutes a literary life:

- continued learning
- improving your writing
- meeting mentors and colleagues
- publishing
- participating in the national literary dialogue
- gaining name recognition
- creative writing

The interview process keeps any writer learning, through the critical study of an author's work, the subsequent conversation, and the work of editing the interview. Each of these tasks engages the writer by introducing new ideas and challenges that will in turn inform his own creative work. By asking questions of another writer's work and having those questions answered by the writer herself, a new writer will find validation and support as well as new ways of considering creative challenges. For example, I asked Andrea Barrett why she included actual characters from history in her fiction, and I learned that this helped her to create the sense that the story took place in the real world. When I asked Elizabeth McCracken why she set *The Giant's House* in a fictional town, she said:

"I didn't want to be beholden to the geography and the particularities of a specific town . . . and I didn't want to have to be historically accurate. The book has a vaguely fairy-tale feeling to it, and because of that, I wanted it set in an imaginary place."

## Who Is This Book For?

I've had all kinds of creative and professional people attend my workshops, including radio and television broadcasters, songwriters, directors, painters, theater people, and artists interested in interviewing other artists in their fields. I've also had social workers, avid readers, students, and journalists interested in getting more involved in literature and developing their interview skills.

While this book directly addresses the author interview, the principles and techniques outlined here can be applied to any artist interview, with songwriters, directors, screenwriters, playwrights, visual artists, filmmakers, and so on. Anyone interested in conducting interviews with creative people for publication, radio, TV, or film will find the techniques and resources in this book indispensable.

If you are already engaged in the work of interviewing, you will learn specific methods for creating more in-depth interviews that will captivate your particular audience. If you are new to interviewing, this book will take you through each step of the interview process, so that you go into your first interview prepared and comfortable and come out with a publishable piece in your hands and the confidence to continue.

This book is for

- aspiring interviewers in any creative field
- writers and other artists who wish to publish, engage in critical study of an author's work, speak with a favorite artist, or deepen their own creative work
- new writers who wish to participate in the literary community
- journalists who want to improve their interview skills
- radio and TV personalities who want to improve their interview skills
- scholars who wish to engage in author interviews as a source of study
- anyone interested in developing their interview skills

# THE ART OF THE AUTHOR INTERVIEW

# CHAPTER 1

# Getting Started

## Know Yourself

Many factors will go into determining the type of interview you will choose to produce. It's important to understand that it's up to you to decide what kind of work you want to do. In this chapter we'll look at some of the issues involved as you begin to consider the nature and style of interview you would like to develop. You do not have to limit yourself to any one variety. I've written in-depth literary interviews for *The Writer's Chronicle* and brief author profiles for my local paper the *Cape Cod Voice,* and both styles provided positive, enjoyable experiences. Let's look at some of the considerations involved in an author interview.

### Where Do You Want to Publish Your Interviews?

Are you interested in interviewing authors for your local newspaper, for a literary journal such as the *Missouri Review,* for a commercial writers' magazine such as *The Writer,* or for mainstream publications such as *Pages?* Understanding the editorial preferences of each publication that you hope to interest in your work is a critical component in developing an appropriate interview. Editors stress and stress again the importance of reading several issues of their publications before submitting or querying them about your work.

When you are thinking about where you would like to publish, consider these editorial preferences and requirements of the publication:
- the target audience
- the level of literary engagement/sophistication
- editorial style
- special interests
- average word length for an interview or article
- deadlines

The target audience is critical. Who will be reading your interview? Academics? Writers? Avid readers? Everyone? It's your job to develop an interview that engages your audience without speaking over their heads or talking down to them. I've found that in publishing for my local paper, a certain level of sophistication was appreciated as long as statements were illustrated with quotes. Ask yourself what will interest your target audience about this author. Will it be the technical aspects of her craft? The story of how she came to write a particular book? Discussion about her involvement in local politics, her experiences in publishing, or some other aspect of her life or work?

If you're writing a piece for your local or regional paper, find out if the author will be in the area and what, if anything, her affiliation or association with your area is. Perhaps she lives in the area and that informs her work in some way, or she has some history or association with the area that you can include for local interest. If it's your decision whom to interview, you will want to bring authors to the table whom your audience will enjoy and benefit from.

Some editors have specific preferences, and understanding them before you submit your work is critical to saving time and avoiding unnecessary worries. For example, Laurence Goldstein of *Michigan Quarterly Review* prefers literary interviews in which the interviewer confronts the author about his ideas or the specific notions presented in his work. Goldstein said recently: "I tend to favor interviews with eminent writers whose work has made a difference in the literary world, in literary history." If you're submitting an interview with a first-time novelist to the *Michigan Quarterly Review*, it will behoove you to know this editorial preference so that you won't expect your wonderful work to be a slam-dunk. Other publications look for interviews with first-time novelists and would more likely appreciate the opportunity to see your work. This is why querying ahead can save time and better focus your expectations.

Other editors, such as John Logan at *Pages* or Kevin Larimer at *Poets & Writers*, look for interviews that will coincide with the release of a book. Therefore, your interview with a writer who's currently in the mountains penning his next great text will not appeal to these editors. If you're interested in publishing in these places, you will need to develop an interview with an author who has an upcoming release. These interviews are usually scheduled two months in advance and require more planning. You first have to be aware of the upcoming release through reading industry magazines such as *Publisher's Weekly*. Then you have to request an advance copy of the book and prepare to conduct your interview before the book actually hits the shelves, so that the publication of your final, edited interview will coincide with the book's release.

Sometimes a publication will have some special interest or angle that they would like you to explore in an interview, especially if the author has local affiliations. If a book is issue related, such as *Middlesex*, which narrates the life of a hermaphrodite and the experiences of his Greek immigrant family in Detroit, an editor may request that you focus on a particular issue-related aspect, such as immigration, Detroit in the budding automotive age, or intersex people.

Most literary journals are interested in high-quality interviews that read as literary pieces on their own. These editors are generally open to interviews with authors of literary distinction, either critically acclaimed or award-winning.

Another consideration for your interview that will depend on where you publish is the expected word length. If you only have five hundred words for a newspaper piece, you're going to create a less in-depth exploration than if you have five thousand words for a literary journal.

Lastly, you need to be aware of the deadline for submitting your interview, and when they will need your comments back on page proofs, so that you can plan your research, compose your questions, and allow time for editing the final interview. Don't accept projects for deadlines that you cannot meet. Missing deadlines can hold up publication and create numerous problems for editors who have their own tight deadlines. If you want to keep working with an editor, you need to make her job as easy as possible by submitting great work on time.

### How and to What Degree Are You Engaged in the Literary Arts?

The literary arts encompass everything from reading your morning paper to reading a detective story or the most recent Pulitzer Prize–winning novel, from writing poems or letters to faraway friends to penning a first novel. The literary arts are broad and diverse and offer something to almost every reader and writer. Determining how and to what degree you're engaged in the literary arts will help you to determine the type of interview you want to do and the best places to publish your work. If you are an avid reader, for example, who is interested in broadening her engagement with the literary arts by conducting an author interview, you will probably not aim for publishing your final piece in *The Writer*. You would be better advised to start publishing for your local or regional newspaper or arts publication and then, when you get some experience and feel more able, you could approach magazines for readers and literary journals.

If you're a published author interviewing other authors, you're well positioned to interview for almost any publication, because you'll have the publishing credentials or name recognition to get you out of the slush pile and into the editor's hands. If you haven't published yet, one of the wonderful benefits of conducting and publishing author interviews is that you gain access to editors, so that they are more likely to read your work and give it serious consideration.

All of this is to encourage you to consider your own abilities and interests as you decide where you would like to publish and what type of interview you would be most comfortable and effective creating.

### Why Do You Want to Interview an Author?

Knowing what you hope to gain for yourself out of conducting an interview can help greatly as you do so. Your reasons for undertaking a given interview project, or for becoming an author interviewer more generally, can be plentiful and varied and change from one moment to the next, but keeping track of them is like taking your pulse—it's a good indication of your literary health in relation to the development of your literary goals. Much of what I'll talk about throughout this book is related to the building of a literary life, without which a writer cannot sustain the work of writing. Taking time to think about the reasons *why* you want to conduct a particular interview will help you extract as much information as you possibly can from the experience. It can also help you step back and take a look at where you are in relation to where you would like to be with your own work and career goals.

It's important to understand your motivations for conducting an interview, regardless of what they are, so that you can make the most out of the interview process and hopefully further your writing and career goals. Some reasons you may want to conduct an author interview:

- you feel that your own work will benefit from the conversation you have with an author
- you have access to an author
- you know that a publication that you're trying to break into is interested in an interview with a specific author
- an author lives in your area and you think you could sell the interview to your local paper
- you've had the writer as a workshop instructor or teacher and think that you can offer a unique perspective on him
- you're familiar with a topic or the themes an author writes about and feel that you could offer a unique exploration of her work

Identifying all of the reasons you have for entering into an interview can help you get the most from the process. In the previous example, by looking at the reason for the interview, we were able to outline the priorities and draw the interviewer's attention to potential opportunities for gaining notice for himself and his work.

### What Has Kept You From Interviewing an Author before Now?

FEAR. Everyone is afraid of famous writers, but no one is more afraid than the person sitting across from them with a tape recorder in her hand,

**Example**

Say you're an emerging writer sending short stories around to a variety of journals and wallpapering your bathroom with a colorful selection of rejections,
some with friendly notes—"Not this time. Try again!"—which keeps you in a
constant state of slapping stamps on envelopes and sending your precious cargo
off to another slush pile. You've decided to do some interviews in the hopes of
publishing them and gaining the attention of some editors who may be interested
in your creative work. If this is the case, you want your interview to demonstrate
  • **your level of professionalism,** as demonstrated by the physical
    presentation of your work and the depth of knowledge and thought it
    displays
  • **a distinctive voice,** as demonstrated through a carefully written biogra-
    phical note and lyrical, provocative, well-informed questions
  • **your commitment to your writing,** as displayed by your efforts and
    thoughtfulness in creating an in-depth interview
  • **your credentials,** in your own bio included with the interview
  Now the occasion of publishing an author interview takes on new dimensions, as it can help you gain access to editors. I've had experiences in which the
editor of a prestigious literary journal has enjoyed my interviews so much that
she's asked to see my fiction, while other editors, through their familiarity with
my interviews, will read the work I send to them so that I bypass the slush pile.
Editors are busy and get a lot of unsolicited manuscripts. For any writer, finding
ways to gain a reputation will be crucial to getting work into the hands of editors who will seriously consider it.

one sweaty finger about to press "record." We're afraid of writers because they're smart and successful, and we interviewers are also afraid
that we're not up to the task. The good news is that if you do your homework and follow the guidelines and instructions that I offer here, you will
be more than up to the task. In fact, you will be way ahead of most professional journalists, who squeeze interviews between lunch and writing
book reviews and haven't even had time to read the author's work. The
only thing to understand about fear is that it's normal. The author you're
about to interview is nervous, too. Like you, he's afraid of sounding stupid, of saying the wrong thing, of having to talk to someone who hasn't
read his work, doesn't seem interested in real issues, or is going to ask unrelated personal questions. Two things that can protect you from fear are
knowing that you've done your homework and that you're well armed
with provocative questions and getting in there and doing it.

  WRITERS AREN'T ACCESSIBLE. Another reason many people interested in interviewing authors never get started is that they believe that
writers are inaccessible. While some are, most aren't. In the next section

we'll talk about how to contact writers and approach them in a way that instills confidence and trust. As you get into this work, you'll realize that there are writers everywhere waiting to be interviewed—at universities and colleges, conferences and retreats, local bookstores, and libraries.

I'M NOT SMART ENOUGH. If you can read and put sentences together, if you finish a book and have genuine questions that you would ask the author if you could, then you are smart enough. Doing an author interview is not rocket science. It takes a commitment to the process, to conducting a respectable amount of research and preparing yourself for the conversation. If you take the tools in this book and put them to work, you'll develop a wonderful author interview. Remember, our questions only have to draw the author out and get her talking. It's her voice that is the star of the show, her voice that will ultimately dazzle your readers. Your job is to set that voice in motion.

Knowing yourself—your own interests, your goals, your engagement in literature—will help you better understand where you fit into the world of author interviews. By asking yourself the critical questions outlined above, you will get the most from your interview experience:

- Where do you want to publish your interviews?
- How and to what degree are you engaged in the literary arts?
- Why do you want to interview an author?
- What has kept you from interviewing an author before?

### Choosing the Author

Where you are in your interviewing career, and what your particular interests are, will influence your decision about which authors to interview. However, there are a few considerations that are always important regardless.

Always interview someone whose work you admire or who raises real questions for you. Remember, you'll be spending a significant amount of time conducting research and reading this author's books, interviews, reviews, and articles, so you want this work to serve your own interests and purposes as well. If your interests are in literary fiction, then you wouldn't interview a romance novelist like Nora Roberts; if you're a science fiction fan, you probably wouldn't be interested in a fiction writer like Ann Patchett. The interview should be informative but also fun, a completely engaging endeavor for you. Who you decide to interview will set the tone for your experience, perhaps in unexpected ways.

**It's Up to the Interviewer**

- Which authors are you most interested in interviewing?
- Which authors would you be less interested in but still willing to interview?
- Which authors do you have no interest in interviewing?

*Your First Interview*

If this is your first author interview, I recommend starting with someone you have access to, such as a teacher, a friend, or a local writer known for supporting the work of new writers. I conducted my first interview with Lynn Freed, my instructor at the Bennington Writing Seminars while I was in the M.F.A. program there. I chose Lynn because I knew her, and through working with her I felt that I had unique insights into what she had to offer other writers in terms of craft and experience. I went on to interview my other instructors, Jill McCorkle and Betsy Cox, and then Elizabeth McCracken, with whom I'd studied at the Provincetown Fine Arts Work Center. Starting with someone you know or someone who travels in your circles will help you feel at ease as you go through your first interview experiences.

*Use Your Connections*

Once I had interviewed people I knew personally, I approached people that I could reach through a mutual connection. For example, my former teacher Doug Bauer introduced me to Sue Miller, who usually doesn't do interviews but agreed to an interview with me as a favor. I had contact with Amy Bloom through a mutual friend, and this small association made me less of a stranger and so increased the chances of her agreeing to an interview. Similarly, Ann Patchett agreed to an interview with me on the recommendation of her good friend Elizabeth McCracken, whom I had already interviewed.

In your quest to interview authors of distinction, ask your teachers, local bookstore owners, or other writers who they know or could put you in touch with for an interview.

*Use Your Credentials*

After you publish a few interviews, you will have established credentials that will help you secure interviews with a wider range of authors. The more you can do to gain an author's trust, the more likely you will be to get a positive response. The types of things that gain an author's trust also demonstrate your commitment to the literary life, such as

- previous publications
- educational background
- teaching affiliations
- awards
- professional experience related to literature (arts administration, etc.)
- personal connections in the field

These credentials make it possible for you to approach writers with whom you have no personal connection—in other words, on the basis of your credentials alone. Credentials open the range of possibilities for you as an interviewer and makes it feasible for you to contact almost any author you want to reach through his publicist or agent.

Choose an author about whom you want to learn more, one whose work you want to read, and one whom you feel would be a benefit to your own creative work, helping to answer the questions that drive you. In considering which author to interview, start with people in your immediate circle, such as your teachers who are published, friends who have published books, and local writers in your area. Once you exhaust the writers in your midst, reach out to writers through mutual connections. Perhaps a writer you interviewed could put you in touch with another interesting author, or your M.F.A. instructor is friendly with someone you've been dying to interview. Don't be afraid to ask for a referral or an introduction.

Finally, you can develop the credentials that will win the trust and interest of authors as they consider which interviews will be worth their time and which ones will not.

### Making Contact with the Author

Your query letter is your first opportunity to present yourself to the author in a professional manner. (See the next section for details on composing a successful query letter.) If you do not have direct access to the author, you can reach him or her through a publicist or agent.

#### Through the Publicist or Agent

To reach an author's publicist, follow these steps:

- Look for the name of the publisher in the front of the author's most recent book.

- Call information for the number of the publisher.
- Call the publisher and ask for publicity at the main switchboard. If your author is under an imprint, for example, Ecco at Harper Collins, ask for Ecco publicity.
- When the publicity department answers the phone, ask for your author's publicist.
- Tell the publicist that you're interested in interviewing the author and explain where you expect to publish the interview. Ask them where you can fax or email your query. I find that email is the most expedient means for communicating with publicists, as they're often in meetings and not available by phone.
- Send your query right after the phone call, while it's fresh in the publicist's mind.
- If the author agrees (authors usually respond in twenty-four to forty-eight hours), the publicist will send you the most recent book and a press kit.
- When you're ready for the interview, contact the publicist and make a date to talk with or meet the author.

Keep in mind that when an author has a new book released, she is looking for publicity opportunities, and her publicist will be eager to help you. If not, you should contact the agent:

- If you don't know who the author's agent is, call the publicist as outlined above and ask.
- Call the agent and let him know that you're interested in interviewing the author, and explain where you expect to publish the interview. Ask the agent where to fax or email your query. Again, email is the most expedient means for communicating with agents, as they're often in meetings and not available by phone.
- Send your query right after the phone call, while it's fresh in the agent's mind.
- If the author agrees (authors usually respond in twenty-four to forty-eight hours), the agent will put you in touch to work out the details.

### The Query Letter

Regardless of how you will be reaching the author, you will need to compose a professional, concise query letter requesting the interview. Even if you know an author personally, as a student or a friend, or through a mutual connection, it's important to make your interviewing relationship a professional one. I do not recommend approaching an author about an interview in a casual way. When the author receives a formal query letter from you, it places the ensuing interview and the discussion surrounding

**Sample Query Letter**

SARAH ANNE JOHNSON
Street
City, State Zip
Phone

Dear Nora Okja Keller:
I'm writing to request an interview with you to be included in a book called *Conversations with American Women Writers*. The collection currently includes Aimee Bender, Amy Bloom, Elizabeth Cox, Elizabeth McCracken, Maria Flook, Lynn Freed, Chitra Banerjee Divakaruni, Sue Miller, Gish Jen, Jill McCorkle, and Jayne Anne Phillips.

The interviews are an in-depth look at the breadth of each author's work, focusing on issues of craft and process, influences, as well as the writer's life. You would be an invaluable addition to this series of interviews with some of today's most critically acclaimed women writing fiction. The interview can be conducted in person, by phone, or by email, whichever is most convenient for you.

I'm a nationally recognized author interviewer and fiction writer with an M.F.A. from the Bennington Writing Seminars. My interviews have appeared in AWP's *The Writer's Chronicle* and *The Writer*, and *GlimmerTrain Stories* has purchased the rights to excerpt from most of these interviews. I have fiction in the spring/summer issue of *Other Voices*. I was Permissions Editor and Senior Researcher on *Best American Movie Writing 2001*, and I currently work as the Program Coordinator for the YMCA National Writer's Voice program and as Project Consultant for the Sundance Institute Arts Writing Program. You can learn more about me at my website: www.sarahannejohnson.com.

Thank you for taking the time to consider this interview. I look forward to hearing back from you soon.

Best Regards,
Sarah Anne Johnson

the interview in the context of a professional request. The query letter shows the author respect and demonstrates that you've formulated cogent reasons for why you are interested in the interview and why you are a good candidate to conduct it; you can also explain where it will be published. The query letter (by email, fax, or mail) also takes the pressure off. If an author is put in the position of having to give you an answer on the spot, she may say "no" just because it's easier and why should she say yes? The letter gives the author time to understand your intentions and to consider whether or not the interview is right for her at the time of the query.

### Deconstructing the Query Letter

Learning to write an effective query letter is critical to securing an interview, and to the success of any writer. Whenever we submit short stories, essays, or poems, or initiate contact with an agent or editor, it is through a query letter. Taking the time to learn to write a thoughtful query letter can mean the difference between seeing your work in print and never having it reach the hands of an editor.

Let's look at each component of the query letter in the above example in order to understand how the letter works.

- *The heading* consists of contact information so that the person reading the query can get back to you. This is essential! An astounding number of queries are sent out each day without contact information. Imagine an editor in love with your interview who is not able to reach you to publish the work.
- *The salutation* is the "Dear Nora Okja Keller" line of the letter. Never use "To whom it may concern" or "Dear Editor." Always find out the name of the person who will be receiving the letter. It shows respect and professionalism to address them by name. (If you don't know an editor's name, call the publication and ask.)
- *The statement of purpose* is in the first paragraph.

    I state my purpose in the line "I'm writing to request an interview with you to be included in a book called *Conversations with American Women Writers*."

    I mention that the interview will be published in a book in the hopes of gaining the author's interest.

    I name the other distinguished authors in the book in the hopes of clinching the deal. After all, the author wants to know the company she will be keeping.
- *The nature of the interview* is described in the next paragraph.

    I describe the type of interview: "an in-depth look at the breadth of each author's work, focusing on issues of craft and process, influences, as well as the writer's life."

    I place the author in the context of the project I'm writing about: "You would be an invaluable addition to this series of interviews with some of today's most critically acclaimed women writing fiction."

    And I give the author the option of how to conduct the interview: "The interview can be conducted in person, by phone, or by email, whichever is most convenient for you."

- *My own biographical note* is in the next-to-last paragraph. Your biographical note is there to instill confidence in the author that you are a professional literary writer. You may only have an M.F.A. and a single publication, but those demonstrate a commitment to the work. Your bio should include your previous related publications, related educational experience, related professional experience, and anything else that will help the author feel comfortable with your expertise.

    My education and background: "I'm a nationally recognized author interviewer and fiction writer with an M.F.A. from the Bennington Writing Seminars."

    My publications: "My interviews have appeared in AWP's *The Writer's Chronicle* and *The Writer*, and *GlimmerTrain Stories* has purchased the rights to excerpt from most of these interviews. I have fiction in the spring/summer issue of *Other Voices*."

    My related job experience: "I was Permissions Editor and Senior Researcher on *Best American Movie Writing 2001*, and I currently work as the Program Coordinator for the YMCA National Writer's Voice program and as Project Consultant for the Sundance Institute Arts Writing Program."

    Other useful information: "You can learn more about me at my website: www.sarahannejohnson.com."

- *The thank you* is the next-to-last element. As a matter of courtesy, you want to thank the author for her time and consideration.
- The closing salutation is the final element. Always sign your letter.

My students often balk at writing their own biographical notes for fear that they have nothing to say that will sell them to an author. I'm including some student query letters here to demonstrate creative options for new author interviewers who do not have previous credentials.

In the first example, the student uses the credentials of her instructor and the fact that the interview is part of her creative writing program to help gain the trust of the author. Finding a way to frame your request so that your lack of experience isn't a factor is a wonderful way around the problem, but it isn't the only way.

The second paragraph, which I suggested the student delete, pertains to the interviewer's creative life, which is not the subject of the interview. The interview is about the author being interviewed and all questions should be focused toward that end. The only thing the interviewer needs to include in the letter about herself are her relevant credentials, as outlined in my sample biographical note above.

**Student Example 1\***

Dear Author:
I'm writing to request an interview with you. As a student in Lesley University's M.F.A. in Creative Writing Program, I will be working with a professional "author interviewer" to learn how to conduct in-depth literary author interviews. I was hoping to conduct my first interview with you as part of the interdisciplinary aspect of my curriculum.

~~I am very interested not only in the subjects you write about but also in how you navigate the delicate terrain of creative nonfiction, my chosen genre and focus of study. Like you, my family's history has been deeply touched by the Holocaust. I am currently working on a piece that explores my father's history while at the same time examining the subtle ways in which his life and experience have impacted my own. I am in the process of reading *Where She Came From* and I am struck by your ability.~~

The interview will explore several aspects of your craft and creative life as a writer. I'm interested in your ability to weave together factual research with your own memories and insights to create an emotionally compelling narrative. I wonder how psychologically difficult a task this writing process is when you are exploring subjects so close to home. I am also curious to hear your thoughts on how wedded one must be to the facts when writing memoir, and how you feel your background in journalism enhances (or doesn't) your ability to write creative nonfiction.

Once I've transcribed and edited the interview, you will receive a draft to clarify and provide feedback where necessary. My goal is to develop a publishable interview for submission to a literary journal such as *AGNI* or the *Harvard Review*.

I would like to conduct the interview in mid to late November as that would provide me with enough time to finish reading your works and prepare appropriate questions.

Thanks very much for your consideration. I look forward to hearing back from you soon. I can be reached at (000) 000–0000 or at <your email address>.

Best,
Student Name

\*Letter courtesy of Amy Yelin.

In the next paragraph, the student does a great job of letting the author know that she is already engaged in the author's work and deeply interested in this conversation and the many directions it could take. Her explanation of the nature of the interview she hopes to pursue is quite likely to capture the interest of the author for several reasons:

- It demonstrates knowledge of the author's work.
- The interviewer is aware of the writer at work, and of her craft.
- She has thought-provoking questions for the author: "I wonder how psychologically difficult a task this writing process is when you are exploring subjects so close to home."
- The interviewer has real literary concerns, such as "how wedded one must be to the facts when writing memoir."

Next, the student sets up expectations, such as how the process of the interview will unfold, what she intends to do with the finished piece, and when the interview will take place. She also includes her contact information.

Just for the record, this particular student tracked down the author's email address because she knew that the author taught at Harvard University. She emailed her final query and received a positive response the same day.

In the first paragraph of the second example, the student states her purpose and indicates the nature of the interview by letting the author know where she hopes to publish it. She also draws a personal connection by letting him know that she saw him at a recent event, which is a very nice touch.

The second paragraph indicates the nature of the interview and some of the topics the interviewer would like to discuss with the author. Its specificity lends clarity of purpose, demonstrating that the interviewer has considered her subject and is well positioned for this interview.

The third paragraph is the interviewer's bio, which lists publishing and teaching credits related to this request. The interviewer closes with a nod to the good use the interview will be put to in the hands of new writers, and a thank-you to the author for considering the request.

While this interviewer doesn't have extensive credentials, she's presented herself in a professional manner, creating a sense of credibility that is likely to help an author agree to an interview.

### Developing a Query Letter Template

Once you've written a query letter or two, it's easy enough to develop a query letter template into which you can plug the relative information. I created the sample query letter to Nora Okja Keller from a template letter

**Student Example #2***

Dear Author,
I'm writing to request an in-depth interview with you for publication in a literary journal such as *The Writer's Chronicle* or *Northwest Review*. I've admired your writing for years, and I enjoyed your reading at the Music of Words event in Bend a couple of years ago.

The interview would focus on your stories and essays, as well as the issues of craft and process that you face as a writer in two genres. I'd also like to talk with you about what it means to be writing from and in the northwest. I've included a few sample questions at the end of this letter.

I hold an M.F.A. from the Bennington Writing Seminars. My creative nonfiction has appeared in *Northwest Review* and *Oregon Home,* and my interview with Kim Barnes will appear in the January issue of *Northwest Review.* I've taught creative writing at Central Oregon Community College.

I hope that you'll consider this conversation for the benefit of new writers, who will look to it for their own learning and inspiration.

Thank you for taking the time to consider this interview. I look forward to hearing back from you soon.

Best,
Student Name

*Letter courtesy of Ellen Santasiero.

that I used to query all of the authors I interviewed for *Conversations with American Women Writers*. Each time I used the letter, I modified the information as needed to best attract a given author.

Making contact with an author is not as daunting a task as it may seem at first. You can locate an author through his publicist or agent; or if he teaches, you can also reach him at his school.

Always make contact through a formal query letter requesting an interview, even if you know the author personally. Whether you're writing, faxing, or emailing the publicist, agent, or author himself, the query letter gives you the opportunity to present yourself in a professional manner, and to indicate the type of interview you'd like to do. It gives the author the chance to make an informed decision based on the content of your letter.

Once you've developed a query letter that works for you, it's a simple matter to turn that letter into a template that you can use for other occasions. This query letter template can become part of the regular resources you use as part of your interview process.

# CHAPTER 2

# The Real Work Begins

Can the interview as a form pass beyond the realm of necessary small talk into art itself? Perhaps. Whenever a good writer uses words, literature is a possibility.

—Wilfried Sheed, *Writers at Work, Fourth Series*

## Conducting the Research

The difference between a good interview and a great interview is primarily one thing: the interviewer's preparation. If you do the requisite research, not only will you be ready for whatever comes up in your conversation with the author, but you will be able to take the conversation in unexpected directions, leading your author into thought-provoking dialogue that reveals the intimacies of her writing process, her creative life, her failures and successes, and anything else you're inspired to pursue.

The first thing students ask is "How long does the research take?"

The answer depends on what you're willing and able to do. For an in-depth literary interview, I recommend giving yourself at least a month of preparation time given that you will have other work or projects going on at the same time. First, this will allow you the time and space to immerse yourself in the author's work. Second, if you give yourself a generous amount of time, you can relax and not rush through the process. The more you enjoy your research, the more you will benefit from it, and the better your interview will be.

If you're under a deadline and simply cannot allow this amount of time, make a tighter schedule and stick to it. Any research is better than no research, and if you internalize the techniques covered in this book, you'll be able to create the elements that will lead to a good interview.

Also, once you've done a few interviews, you'll go through the re-

*Epigraph.* Wilfried Sheed, introduction to *Writers at Work, Fourth Series* (New York: Penguin Books, 1977)

search phase faster because your mind will be attuned to what you need in order to compose your questions and conduct the interview. Your research will be better focused as you gain experience.

There are two aspects involved in conducting the research for an author interview: one-time research about a specific author, and ongoing research related to author interviews in general.

### Researching the Author

First, you must research the author—his books, essays, articles; reviews about his work; articles or profiles about him. Search online, go to libraries, and read everything you can find.

With your *writer's eye* read *all* of his books in his main genre and any other genres he writes in. Reading with your writer's eye means looking under the hood at how the engine of their writing operates. How do they create scenes, handle transitions, draw characters, create tension, or address other aspects of the craft? What themes do they explore? What locations do they frequent? Make notes as you read. Underline, scribble in the margins, whatever it takes to engage your mind in asking questions of the work. How are they achieving the effect of the novel?

Read all of the articles or essays written by the author as well. You can search for these online or in the library, or you can ask the author for samples of essays or articles that he's written. Most often, a writer's work outside his genre reflects interests that are critical to his creative work. For instance, Lynn Freed has written essays about her experiences as a Jewish South African woman, a theme in all of her novels, as well as articles about travel, which inform her writing life in that she's a writer who writes away from home:

Home is an idea, and it is past tense. I am someone who makes a home out of a hotel room. The minute I arrive, I start arranging things to make the place my own. I have felt at home on a dhow on the Nile, and I have not felt at home in a house in which I lived in San Francisco for fourteen years. There is something beyond reason in the places that resonate. I am more likely, for instance, to feel at home with the sound and sight of the sea than in the most idyllic setting inland—which is where I happen to live now. I long for the sea. Why don't I just pack up and move? There is a question I can't seem to answer. Ennui, I suppose. (Sarah Anne Johnson, *Conversations with American Women Writers* [Hanover, N.H.: University Press of New England, 2004], 83)

Read all of the articles and interviews *about* your author. Writings about your author can help you to articulate vagaries in your own thinking, lead you into areas you'd like to pursue further with the author, and elucidate ideas and themes you hadn't previously considered. Additionally, reading other articles and interviews with your author will familiarize you with the writer and prepare you for the interview, as well as inform you about what the author has already said or been asked in interview after interview. There is nothing more annoying to writers than to be asked the obvious questions that they have already answered countless times. If you have to ask a redundant or obvious question because your editor requires it or your interview will be incomplete without it, try to find a different angle on the question. (See "Questions That Ask the Obvious" later in this chapter)

Read all of the reviews you can about your author's work. The *New York Times Book Review* website at www.nytimes.com/books has an online searchable database that goes back several years. Like articles and interviews with your author, book reviews will familiarize you with others' opinions about the author's books and may point out themes or issues you hadn't previously considered. You can usually find thought-provoking quotes in reviews that will provide good leads into questions.

In the following pages, I've provided worksheets in which you can list resources on your interview subject, and space in which to make notes on each resource for future use. If you photocopy these pages, you can have them for ongoing use as you conduct your interviews.

1. List the author's books you intend to read and make any relevant notes:

_____

_____

_____

_____

_____

_____

2. List articles or essays written *by the author* that you'll read for your interview:

_____

_____

_____

_____

_____

_____

3. List articles and interviews *about the author* that you'll read for your interview:

_____

_____

_____

_____

_____

_____

4. List reviews about your author's work:

_____

_____

_____

_____

_____

*Ongoing Research*

You must always be procuring, reading, and filing away articles, essays, interviews, or books on the craft of writing to help you compose insightful, thought-provoking questions. I've compiled a list of some of the resources I regularly consult and provided space for you to develop a list of your own.

Some of my favorites include the following:

- books on craft: *The Writer's Chapbook*, edited from the *Paris Review* interviews, with an introduction by George Plimpton; *Bird by Bird*, by Anne Lamott; *One Writer's Beginnings*, by Eudora Welty; and *Burning Down the House*, by Charles Baxter
- writing magazines: *The Writer's Chronicle, The Writer, Poets & Writers*
- magazines for readers: *Pages, Speakeasy, Bloomsbury Review, Ruminator Review, Bookmarks*
- literary or arts journals: *Paris Review, Agni, Mississippi Review, Other Voices, GlimmerTrain Stories, Provincetown Arts* (see the last pages of *Best American Short Stories* for a listing of one hundred literary journals)
- Websites: salon.com, pifmagazine.com, nytimes.com/books, identitytheory.com

1. List your five favorite books on the craft of writing:

_____

_____

_____

_____

_____

_____

2. List your five favorite magazines related to writing/reading:

_____

_____

_____

_____

_____

_____

3. List your five favorite literary journals:

_____

_____

_____

_____

_____

4. List your five favorite online resources:

_____

_____

_____

_____

_____

Conducting thorough research of your author and her work is critical to developing an in-depth interview. If you do not have as much time as you would like to conduct your research, set aside as much time as you can manage and decide which aspects of the research will best serve your interview.

Ideally, your research will include reading the following:
- all of the author's work in his/her genre (at least the last three books)
- all of the author's work outside his/her genre
- all of the author's articles/essays/etc.
- other articles and interviews with the author
- reviews of the author's work

In addition to the specific research you conduct for your interview, you should always be reading books and magazines that will inform your thinking and make you aware of interesting lines of questioning, current trends, issues of craft, and so on. Additionally, watching interviews on television such as *Inside the Actor's Studio* or listening to radio interviews such as *Fresh Air* with Terry Gross can help you get a feel for how different interviewers conduct an interview—when they listen, when they interject, how they handle the role of interviewer, and what their questions are like. This ongoing research will include

- books on craft
- writing magazines
- magazines for readers
- literary or arts journals
- websites
- television interviews with creative people such as actors, writers, and dancers
- radio interviews with creative people

## Composing the Questions

Composing the questions for your interview gets at the heart of the direction your interview will take. Here's where all of your research and the time that you took to immerse yourself in the author's world come together and begin to pay off. Good interview questions that demonstrate a firm grasp of an author's work and a genuine interest in conversation about that work will surely lead to a great interview. In his introduction to the first series of *Writers at Work* in 1957, Malcolm Cowley said of previous author interviews:

Most of the interviewers either have had no serious interest in literature or else have been too serious about themselves. Either they have been reporters with little knowledge of the author's work and a desire to entrap him into making scandalous remarks about sex, politics, and God, or else they have been ambitious writers trying to display their own sophistication, usually at the expense of the author, and listening chiefly to their own voices.

He goes on to describe the interviews in *Writers at Work* as being "of a different order."

They [the interviewers] have done their assigned reading, they have asked the right questions, or most of them, and have listened carefully to the answers. The authors, more conscious of their craft than authors used to be, have talked about it with an engaging lack of stuffiness . . . It tells us what fiction writers are as persons, where they get their material, how they work from day to day, and what they dream of writing.

In a sense, Cowley has provided fodder for any interviewer considering what to ask his interview subject: where she gets her ideas, what her writing routine is like, and so on. But more importantly, he outlines the pitfalls: poor preparation and showcasing one's own literary prowess rather than the author's. Since the questions will set the tone and direction of your interview, they are the place where you can begin to avoid the pitfalls that nearly half a century later still hold true of most author interviews. You've done your homework, and now you will continue your preparation by developing questions that seek to draw your author into conversation.

### The Role of the Interview Questions

It's important to remember that the interview questions are not vehicles for showcasing your own knowledge but rather for generating discussion and creating a forum in which the author can talk about her own work. David Sherwin, former managing editor at AWP's *The Writer's Chronicle*, reminds us, "The interviewer is there as a facilitator, not a celebrity, and their role should stay as such—out of the limelight."

Your interview questions should reveal the writer you are interviewing and all that he has to offer your intended audience. Your questions should
  • draw out the interesting aspects of the author's work;
  • look at the author's breadth of work, as well as particulars about specific works;
  • explore recurring themes, influences, and issues in the author's work;
  • paint the background of the author's career and place any new work in context;
  • ask specific questions about the new book being promoted;
  • ask any questions of particular interest to your target audience; and
  • list previous works, awards, and teaching affiliations.

One of the most important aspects of composing questions is keeping the conversation in the context of literature. This means that all of your questions must seek to expose the writer at work and explore issues of craft or subjects in the author's work. Questions about the author's favorite television shows, for example, are irrelevant unless you can tie the question to the author's work in some way. If you find yourself wanting to ask a question unrelated to writing, then find a way to tie it into the literary context of the interview. How does what you're asking about inform the author's work? If you're going to ask about the author's favorite television show, for example, tie the experience of watching television to the author's creative life. "What is your favorite television show? Does television inspire your creative life, or does it provide escape?"

If you place your questions in the context of literature, you will be able to ask almost anything. One of the biggest problems I see in student interviews is the lapse into a line of inquiry that is not in the realm of literature and is therefore off topic.

### Remember Your Audience

Remember that you are writing this interview for an intended audience. The questions in an interview written for *The Writer's Chronicle* will be very different from those you'd ask in an interview for your local paper. For instance, in the *Pacific Sun* (December 24, 1997) Jill Kramer asks Lynn Freed the following questions:

- What was it like growing up in South Africa?
- Was there much of a Jewish community?
- In *Home Ground* you write that even in the fifties there was a sense among whites that a revolution was coming.
- Is your family still there?
- Tell me about your years at Columbia during the student protests.

These questions are of general interest, focusing on the personal, the political, and the global but not on Lynn Freed's work or her writing life. While these questions are not asked in the context of literature, they could easily be cast into the context of literature.

- What was it like growing up in South Africa? *How does that experience inform your fiction?*
- In *Home Ground* you write that even in the fifties there was a sense among whites that a revolution was coming. *How does the tension of growing up in a community fraught with racial and political strife inspire your creative life?*

Often local or regional magazines will want the interview to address issues of local interest. In a magazine such as *The Writer's Chronicle* the interviewer is free to ask deeper questions about the author's life and work as well as questions that are geared to an audience of writers rather than the general public. Here are some questions from the Lynn Freed interview in *The Writer's Chronicle* that came out last summer:

I recently enjoyed a short-short you published in *The Atlantic Monthly* called "Lovely, Lovely." Could you talk about the form of the short-short and what you're trying to achieve in that small space of narrative?

In reading through your novels, starting with *Heart Change, Home Ground,* then moving on through *The Bungalow,* and *The Mirror,* one can see the development of your craft. You've often referred to *Heart Change* as a "teething novel." How would you describe the others in terms of what you struggled with or sought to develop by way of craft?

Let's talk about some of the themes that recur in your work. First, there's the setting in South Africa, your native land. One senses the longing and nostalgia for home, yet the characters so often want to leave South Africa for other lands. Is this aspect of your fiction autobiographical? Can you comment on this?

Also a theme in your work is the woman striving to define herself amidst a society that wants to place her into a restrictive, traditional role. Your women characters are seeking fulfillment through education, love, sex, adventure, enterprise, and so on. Comment?

These questions seek to reveal the writer at work by exploring issues of craft, the writer's development, themes, and so on. These questions would also be of interest to an audience of readers. Magazines for readers such as *Pages* and *Speakeasy* offer room for deeper exploration of a writer's work as well.

Reading other interviews in the publication in which you'd like to place your interview will give you a feel for what's appropriate and also expose you to different types of questions, giving you ideas for your own interview. Building substantial questions that go beyond one line and offer quotes or interesting information for the writer to react to will prove interesting for both the author and the reader, who may or may not have read the author's books.

The interview below with Jonathan Lethem for the *Brooklyn Rail* offers an excellent example of an interview that gets at some of the heart of the book and the author at work while addressing local issues.*

**Theodore Hamm (*Rail*):** Your story is set against the backdrop of gentrification. We're sitting here in Halcyon on Smith Street, a café that sells music along with '70s furniture. Did you ever think that when you were growing up around here in the '70s that your neighborhood would become trendy?

**Jonathan Lethem:** Smith Street for me focuses the paradox of gentrification so intensely. In the book I manage to reclaim a lot of the territory, and locate my affection for the Smith Street of my childhood. But in practical terms, Smith Street was a place that I was mostly trying to never be caught dead on. It was the gauntlet I ran on my way home from P.S. 93, my junior high school. So when I look at these restaurants—which I'm enjoying as much as anyone—the first thing I think is that even if I wasn't from here, it's exactly

---

*"In Conversation, Jonathan Lethem with Theodore Hamm," *The Brooklyn Rail* (October 2003). Over the summer of 2003, Jonathan Lethem spoke to the *Rail* about *Fortress of Solitude*, his sixth novel.

where someone like me would now be living anyway. By the time I finished the book, I found a way to embrace the contradictions of gentrification. I came to understand that the wish to live in a society that is classless, and that doesn't disenfranchise anyone, is beautiful and poignant but also hopeless—and it absolutely won't be solved on a block-by-block basis.

*Rail:* In writing the work, did you consciously resist any inclinations toward nostalgia about the neighborhood?

**Lethem:** Yes, because Boerum Hill has always been a patchwork, where different classes and cultures were rubbing against one another. It's a zone of permanent transition. There used to be rooming houses where sailors and longshoremen lived, and there were Mohawk bars, near where American Indian workers lived. It was an incredible place to come to consciousness because it forced you into so much awareness of the contradictions. Turn any corner, like the one from Dean Street to Nevins Street, and a whole new set of meaning arises.

*Rail:* Is there a line between memoir and fiction in the book?

**Lethem:** It's not one that I can draw for you, but I did want the portrait of the milieu—the neighborhood itself—to be almost documentary. Not that there aren't fictional aspects or places where I fudge dates. I compressed the gentrification of Gowanus so as to bring it all under Dylan's witnessing eye. But for people who know the area, I wanted it to be a real portrait as well. Similarly, the characters are fictional composites, fragmentary representations of people I've known. The book invites a lot of speculation on the autobiographical elements because they are in there. It's most germane to point out, for instance, that I don't see myself only in Dylan, but I see big parts of myself in Abraham—his art making is really kind of a confession of a novelist's trudging work. There are big chunks of me in Arthur Lomb as well. But the fact of the matter is that there wasn't only one white boy in Gowanus when I was growing up—there were 15 or 20.

*Rail:* I'm wondering how universal you think the story is, at least for those of us who grew up in the 1970s. Personally, I could relate to it, even though I grew up in Evanston, next to Chicago. The town has a fairly large black population, and in your book, Mingus reminded me of some of my friends, whereas I also got my ass kicked by a guy named Rodnes Muckleroy, who is like your Robert Woolfolk.

**Lethem:** I'm glad you can connect with it, but at the same time I hope that it doesn't require any specific framework for it to be legible. Whether a story is universal is the kind of question you should never be asking yourself when you're writing it. For me this book is obviously enormously specific, and intimate. Still, my editor at the *London Review of Books* wrote me a long letter explaining how the book seemed to be about his own childhood in England, and race was not an issue in his school days at all. Maybe it's that the scrupulously personal story I've written invites personal reflection or emotion from the reader—at least that's what I hope for.

**Rail:** Let's talk about the race issues in the book a bit more. Throughout the book you speak authoritatively about the black experience, in both positive and negative ways. Did you feel cautious in this regard, fearing a possible critical backlash?

**Lethem:** I guess that the reason I felt that I could write the book was that I didn't really ever challenge myself to posture or pontificate about anything. I think that it's foremost a book of characters, and so whether they're black or white doesn't matter. It was the way that I worked through these characters and understood their experience individually, rather than as members of any group. In *Girl in Landscape,* I wrote a book from the point of view of a 13-year-old girl, and people would ask me how I thought I had the ground to stand on, to write from that point of view. I knew that if my project was to write from the female point of view per se, I'd be completely paralyzed. But my goal was to write about Pella Marsh, a character I invented and created out of big parts of my own emotional landscape.

**Rail:** But in *Fortress,* the main white character ends up a successful writer, and two of the main black characters end up in prison. So you are making a commentary.

**Lethem:** It's a painful commentary, and there's a lot in the book that isn't resolved. It seems to be that the book just barely hints a taste of redemption for everyone involved by the end. But just barely, because I was contemplating things that I don't have the answers to. I just wanted to articulate my sense of the meaning of the questions—of living with the realities I know. And it's not my place to control people's reading of it.

*Types of Questions and Suggestions*

There are numerous types of questions that you can ask any author, some simple and some more complex. Understanding how these questions work, what they will elicit from an author, and what their basic elements are will help you compose your own complex, provocative questions. This section discusses the various types of questions that you can create. Then we'll look at some sample interviews and examine the questions and their basic parts in the interest of decoding erudite questions so that we can learn to assemble our own.

QUESTIONS THAT LOOK AT THE BODY OF WORK. Now that you've read *all* of the author's work, including work outside her usual genre, you can ask questions that step back and look at her work as a whole. What

**Exercise**

Read only the questions in the sample interview with Jonathan Letham. What do you notice? How would you describe the nature of this interview? What does it explore? What does it not explore?

How could you rephrase the questions to place them in a literary context?

The interview is 1000 words, so the interviewer was working with a tight word limit. How do you think he did in terms of getting as much as he could from such a short allotted space?

Now read the entire interview. As you read each question, notice its various components—quotes, anecdotes, examples from text—and ask yourself how you could've composed a more interesting question if you weren't constrained to the 1000-word limit.

Then notice what sort of answer the question elicited from the author. Is it what you expected? If not, how is different, and why do you think that is?

What have you learned from this interview? Is there anything you think would have been more important to ask?

---

do you notice going on? Your knowledge of the author's work will earn her trust and engage her interest in your conversation. The Lynn Freed interview questions include one about the author's body of work: "In reading through your novels, starting with *Heart Change, Home Ground,* then moving on through *The Bungalow* and *The Mirror,* one can see the development of your craft. You've often referred to *Heart Change* as a 'teething novel.' How would you describe the others in terms of what you struggled with or sought to develop by way of craft?"

After having read all of her novels, I stood back and noticed the development of her craft through each successive book. Using a quote of hers, I asked her about the issues she faced. This question wins the author's confidence by

- letting her know that I've read all of her work;
- letting her know that I've studied up on her, as evidenced by the quote; and
- opening the door for her talk about her development as a writer.

The simplest version of this question would be "What challenges did you face in writing each book?" While this simpler version of the question might get the job done, it loses the benefit to the author of feeling "known" by the interviewer, and it doesn't set up the question for the reader, who may or may not have read Freed's work. Posing the question in the context of Freed's development as a writer throughout each successive book introduces to the reader the idea that writers grow and develop. Writers

**Exercise**

Sit back and relax. Take a few deep breaths and imagine asking your author "What challenges did you face in writing each book?"

Now, imagine placing that question in a larger context by offering an observation about what you notice developing throughout their work, or perhaps using a quote from the author or a critic. Now ask, "What challenges did you face in writing each book?"

are not born with a pen in hand spouting lyric phrases, and we want the reader to see how a writer struggles and grows through each book.

QUESTIONS ABOUT WRITING IN GENERAL. There are always general questions about how an author came to writing, what their writing process is like, what they struggle with in terms of craft, and what their other influences might be. These general questions are important and can yield wonderful responses. They also provide a nice lead into an interview, in that they give both the author and the interviewer time to warm up to each other and to the conversation. For example, in the Edna O'Brien interview the interviewer asks a question about how O'Brien came to writing: "If you had always loved literature, why did you study chemistry at university rather than English?"

In *Conversations with American Women Writers* I asked Amy Bloom: "I know that your original career was in psychotherapy. How did you go from psychotherapy to writing?" I then explored the interplay of writing and therapy with the following question: "What role does empathy play in your writing? How does empathy work differently in writing than in your role as a therapist?"

The conditions and situations a writer has experienced often serve their writing in some way, and exploring how a writer got started and what steps they took to develop their craft can lead to wonderful and unexpected answers. For example, when I interviewed Sena Jeter Naslund after the success of *Ahab's Wife,* I asked her how she got started writing and what she did to develop her craft. Sena shared how difficult the craft of writing was for her to learn, how hard she had to work, and how long it took for her to achieve the kind of success she enjoyed with *Ahab's Wife.* Her openness and candor in sharing her failures and early experiences are wonderful gifts to any struggling writer or artist, and it was not what I expected upon asking the question.

QUESTIONS ON THE SPECIFICS OF THE WORK. Having read all of the author's work, you will be able to ask specific questions about particulars too. By zooming in on the specific issues of craft that you detected with your *writer's eye,* you can illustrate for the reader what you see going on in the work and then ask the writer to talk more about how she achieves specific effects or techniques.

In the following example I ask Aimee Bender about a particular aspect of her work: "In 'Fugue' you interweave the stories of several different characters, and number and in some cases title each section. How did you develop this structure or did it emerge as you wrote it?"

This question is easy to take apart because it's a detailed question about a specific structure the author chose for organizing her story. It also explores the larger question of how structure emerges—is it organic or imposed? This question will provoke a twofold answer: (1) whether the structure was organic or imposed, and (2) the author's thinking about the structure.

In *Women Writers at Work,* Sasha Guppy asks Edna O'Brien a well-informed question on the particulars of *Pagan Place:* "Another interesting aspect of that novel is that it is written in the second person singular, like a soliloquy. It is somewhat reminiscent of Molly Bloom's soliloquy in *Ulysses;* were you conscious of the influence?" O'Brien goes on to state that it wasn't Molly Bloom who inspired her use of the second person singular but instead the psychological pressure within the character.

QUESTIONS THAT EXPLORE EXTERNAL INFLUENCES. Another type of question explores external influences on the author's work, such as other writers, childhood experiences, teaching, travel, ethnicity, sexuality, other interests or obsessions—it could be anything at all. For example, Amy Hempel, in her interview with Scottish novelist Alan Warner (*BOMB,* spring 1999), begins: "I find that most writers' dialogue sounds written, not spoken, but yours is uncannily accurate. Does this have something to do with your love of music, or do you just listen closely?" Hempel explores the influence of music on Warner's work while at the same time pursuing a question about craft. This not only makes for an interesting question, it also lets the interview subject know in no uncertain terms that the interviewer has done her homework (for example, she knows about his interest in music).

The following excerpt is from my interview with Lynn Freed in *Conversations with American Women Writers* ([Hanover, N.H.: University Press of New England, 2004], 78). It explores the external influence of the theater on her development as a writer:

**Johnson:** How did growing up in the theater help shape you as a writer? Did it influence your desire to write?

**Freed:** I didn't grow up in the theater itself, but as the daughter of parents who were in the theater. There is a difference. I could never stand to be on stage, at least not literally. But when you grow up in a family like mine, in which performance, both formal and informal, is prized, you're never quite offstage. As the youngest child, I soon found that the way to attract and keep attention was to perform as myself. Not necessarily the self I was—whatever that was—but the self that I divined they might wish me to be. In this case, it was clown—not an uncommon role for the youngest child in such a family.

Lynn's response explains her early relationship to theater and, more importantly, the role of performance in her family and how she adapted herself to that role by playing the clown. I then brought the discussion back to her writing.

**Johnson:** How does that sense of drama work in your fiction?

**Freed:** I would consider a "sense of drama" an aspect of timing. Timing is in the ear. To a certain extent, the ear can be trained—reading, writing, performing (on and off the page). But there is also a sort of innate sense of timing that one is born with. My mother had it; my father didn't. He had to be taught by her. Although she was a woman without an apparent sense of humor, her great gift was comic timing. In this, she was faultless. Her dramatic timing was also very good, but the comic timing was brilliant. Anyway, when I would perform, either on or off the page, it was she who would always call me on the timing. "You're off here," she'd say. Or, "Once is enough." Or, "Cut!" Or, occasionally, "Oh, that is good!" One cannot underestimate the value of such a training, and so early. I still feel her voice as I write.

And that is the technical answer I was after all along. What I've learned through the process of interviewing writer after writer is that one's abilities can be traced back to earliest yearnings and experiences.

Other simple questions about external influences on one's work include:
* How does your reading life influence or inform your writing life?
* What writers first influenced your work?
* Are there other influences on your work?

Researching your writer, reading everything you can find out about them, will help you to learn about their interests and ask well-informed questions about external influences on their writing.

QUESTIONS THAT REQUIRE DIPLOMACY. When faced with difficult questions—say, about an author's shortcomings or failings—exercise diplomacy. Amy Hempel asks Alan Warner: "A number of writers I know feel that a book, as a human document, should be flawed. Are there places where you feel your reach exceeded your grasp? Something you couldn't get exactly?" What a beautiful and generous way to ask a writer about his failures without putting him on the defensive. She places the conversation into the context of writing by citing statements from other writers she knows. This also takes the pressure off Warner, in that she isn't pointing the finger at him and his flaws but discussing a wider issue that all writers face.

Her question *opens up* the conversation. Other ways to pose questions about a writer's failures include:

- What are the challenges you faced in your early work?
- Are there issues of craft that you struggle with now?
- Are there ways in which you're disappointed with a book when it's finally done?
- Does your finished book live up to your expectations?

These are the questions in their simplest form. You can add quotes from other writers or examples from the writer's work to add heft and weight to these simple inquiries and bring them into the larger world of literature and writers.

QUESTIONS THAT USE QUOTES FROM THE AUTHOR'S WORK. Use quotes from the author's text to support or elucidate a question you're asking. For instance, in an interview with Chitra Banerjee Divakaruni, I say:

You also choose physical details that draw your characters quite distinctly and also serve to create an intimacy between the characters and the reader. For example, in *Mistress of Spices:* "Geeta's grandfather still walking like a military major though it has been twenty years. His shirt ironed stiff with pointy collars, his steel-gray pants perfect-creased down the front. His shoes, midnight-black Bata shoes spit-polished to match the onyx he wears on his left hand for mental peace." How do you arrive at these carefully placed details?

The simplest form of this question would be "How do you arrive at the physical details that draw your characters distinctly while also creating an intimacy between the characters and the reader?" Here, the quote provides an example of critical physical details that draw her character so well and give her an immediate reference point from which to speak. The quote makes the question *specific* rather than general and also offers the reader a taste of the author's work and an example of the aspect of craft being discussed, so that the reader, too, has a reference point.

Amy Hempel finishes up her interview with Alan Warner with the following:

This last is not a question so much as a comment. There is a line near the end of *Morvern Callar* that makes me teary every time I read it. There is a night when Morvern goes from rave to wave—she leaves a night of dancing and drugs in a club on Ibiza and finds an unpeopled spot of beach. She goes for a sensuous swim in the sea, in the dark, and then says, "I hadn't slept for three days so I could know every minute of that happiness that I never even dared dream I had the right."

Everything in this question is leading up to that final comment. Here, Hempel selected a quote that's particularly meaningful and evocative to her as a means of eliciting a final response from Warner. She first lets Warner know that the line is a moving one for her, then she sets the scene in which the line occurs. This is a wonderful use of a quote, and as you'll read later, Warner has a great response.

QUESTIONS THAT USE QUOTES FROM OTHER AUTHORS. Use quotes on craft from other writers to engage the author in discussing their work in a larger literary context. In Amy Hempel's interview with Alan Warner, she asks: "My friend, the poet John Rybicki, has one of my favorite descriptions of what it is like to write. He calls it 'lunging at vacancy.' How was writing different for you in *The Sopranos* from what it was to sit down and write *Morvern Caller?*"

This question, in its simplest terms, is "How was writing your second book different from writing your first?" But by including the Rybicki quote, Hempel places the question in the context of literature, rather than confining it to Warner's own experience. Her question also places the interview into a larger literary conversation about writing.

In the interview with Lynn Freed, I ask:

**Johnson:** Richard Ford has said that place is yet another character in your story or novel. Do you agree with this?

**Freed:** No. There is place, and there are characters in the place. Without place, of course, there could be no story, no life, no anything. But place is the ground of the fiction. It is there before the fiction, and after the fiction is over. And it is unchanged. It is the given.

I introduced something I'd heard Richard Ford say in an interview as a means for getting Lynn's opinion on this issue of place in fiction. By having a quote from a distinguished writer, I place the question in the larger literary dialogue that goes on among writers, which gives the question more weight than if I had asked "Do you think of place as a character in your fiction?" Also, the Ford quote lets readers know that this is something that writers talk about and think about; it is an issue in our work. The juxtaposition of two opposing opinions on this issue provides an interesting perspective on how different writers are from one another. It further reinforces what we already know—that every writer works by his or her own set of aesthetics and ideals in much the same way that you will develop your own aesthetics and ideals as an interviewer.

Finding quotes from other writers is as easy as cracking open the latest issue of *Poets & Writers* or *The Writer's Chronicle*, any of the books in the *Writers at Work* interview series, or books on craft such as *Bird by Bird*, by Anne Lamott. This type of reading falls into the category of ongoing general research.

QUESTIONS THAT ASK THE OBVIOUS. Don't be afraid to ask the obvious, as long as you spin the question in a way that makes it interesting. Hempel asks Warner: "Are you sick to death of people asking how you write so convincingly in the voices of young women?" This is clearly a question that he's asked all the time, but by acknowledging this, Hempel not only gets away with asking the question but wins him over by acknowledging how often he's been asked it.

I had the pleasure of interviewing Donna Tartt upon publication of *The Little Friend*, which was released a decade after her international blockbuster *The Secret History*. Ardent fans wanted to know why she took ten years to turn out another novel, and interviewer after interviewer posed this same question, until Tartt became annoyed nearly to the point of infuriation with people harping on this. Tartt's frustration, I imagine, derived from both the lack of awareness on the part of the interviewer about what other interviewers were doing, and also the frame around the question and the question's underlying implications: "What took you so long?"

In being faced with interviewing Tartt for a publication that insisted I pursue the issue of her decade between publications, I decided to take the question further and reframe it: "What went on in the ten-year gestation period during the writing of *The Little Friend*?"

Framed in this manner, the question becomes one of craft. It shows respect for the author's creative process and leads the author into a dialogue about it. Tartt enjoyed the interview, which I took as a great compliment, given how many she had to contend with and how annoying some of them became. Making the effort to step beyond the obvious, in this case, made all the difference.

QUESTIONS THAT EXPLORE THE PERSONAL. If you want to ask something personal, cast it in the light of literary thought, so the author can address the question in terms of literature and not his personal life. For example, if you have a writer who has written a series of poems about a painful divorce, rather than asking "So, sounds like you had a bad divorce?" try something like this: "It seems that much of your material is based on personal experience. How do you maintain a balance between expressing the personal and not letting it overwhelm the work?" Or: "What is the role of autobiography in your poetry?" Pitched as such, these questions draw the writer into thinking and talking about how one pursues potentially volatile material as an artist, whereas a question about a divorce leaves room for not much more than gossip. Hempel gives us another good example when she asks Warner: "You've written about your homeland, but not, it seems, about yourself. Yet your background is certainly compelling—why haven't you gone there on the page? Will you at some time in the future?" She wants to know why he doesn't write about himself, yet she couches her question in a larger literary context, writing about the homeland, writing about the self. Her question leaves room for Warner to offer personal details and address more literary concerns, and he does some of both.

In an interview with Amy Hempel conducted by Paul Winner in the summer 2003 issue of the *Paris Review,* Winner asks: "Does structuring a story that takes its departure from real life pose some technical problems? Doesn't the real event impose its own parameters?" Here the interviewer is asking about personal material, but in the context of a literary dilemma—how to handle autobiographical elements so they don't overwhelm the fiction.

QUESTIONS OF SPECIAL INTEREST. Many publications will request that an interview have an angle or ask specific questions related to special interests, especially local or regional issues related to an author or work. The Jonathan Lethem interview in the *Brooklyn Rail* is a great example of this type of author interview, as it almost exclusively asks questions related to Brooklyn and Lethem's associations and influences with regard to the city. In fact, three of the six questions are about Brooklyn:

- Your story is set against the backdrop of gentrification. We're sitting here in Halcyon on Smith Street, a café that sells music along with '70s furniture. Did you ever think that when you were growing up around here in the '70s that your neighborhood would become trendy?
- In writing the work, did you consciously resist any inclinations toward nostalgia about the neighborhood?
- Is there a line between memoir and fiction in the book? (While this may not appear to be about the city, he's asking if everything in the book, including what's written about Brooklyn, is true.)

I interviewed Marge Piercy for a local newspaper, the *Cape Cod Voice,* and the editor there asked that I make some tie-in's with her life on Cape Cod. I chose to create avenues into Piercy's work through exploring the inspiration she derives from the natural life on Cape Cod, and through asking a question about a recent political issue that she was involved in.

In *Colors Passing through Us,* Piercy's latest book of poetry, Cape Codders will discover a fresh new look at our natural world through the lens of Piercy's personal observations and lyrical descriptions. Readers will find themselves at home with images of foxes, coyotes, sandy dunes, and the bay in poems like "Quieting on the bay" and "Resort offseason." Piercy is a Cape Codder who remains politically active in local issues. She is also devoted to her garden, and passionately engaged in observing our exquisite natural setting. She chose to move to Wellfleet from New York, in search of a healthier way to live, a more beautiful place to live that could nurture and support her creative life, as so many artists and writers do.

Other special interest publications may want you to draw out certain aspects of an author's work as it relates to their interest. For example, an opera magazine could ask a journalist to interview Ann Patchett about her novel *Bel Canto,* with a focus on opera.

## Getting It All on Paper

So far we've covered a lot of information regarding the nature of the questions, the many different types of questions you can ask, and how to use your research to make your questions more substantial. But how do you go about getting it down on paper? Where do you start?

### Step One: Brainstorm

The first step in getting your questions down on paper is to simply start writing. Brainstorm by writing down absolutely everything you can think of that you'd like to ask the author. Don't worry yet about the reader, the questions, the complexity, using quotes, or citing examples from their work, just get everything down. When you've exhausted your own mind, turn to the texts that you read and go through your notes to find any other questions that you ruminated about as you were reading. Look through your notes on other articles and interviews—anything you used to record your thoughts as you were reading—and write down every question you can think of for your author.

### Step Two: Flesh Out Your Raw Material

Now that you have all of your questions, you can begin to flesh them out with quotes and examples from the author's work. This is where you take the question in its simplest form and place it in the larger literary dialogue that continually goes on amongst writers and literary enthusiasts. We've looked at several examples, but let's look again at an excerpt from Amy Hempel's interview with Alan Warner. Say, for example, you're looking at the author's body of work, and you want to know how writing his first novel was different from the experience of writing his most recent novel. During your brainstorm you wrote: "How was writing your first book different from writing your most recent?"

This is the question in its simplest form, which we can improve upon by adding a quote and referring to the novels by name, as Hempel demonstrates: "My friend, the poet John Rybicki, has one of my favorite descriptions of what it is like to write. He calls it 'lunging at vacancy.' How was writing different for you in *The Sopranos* from what it was to sit down and write *Morvern Caller?*"

Something as simple as referring to the book by title can improve the flow of a question and reduce ambiguities. Of course, this unusual quote adds color to the question and raises the level of conversation by placing the question in the context of literature.

### Step Three: Put the Questions in Order

The order of your questions is important, in that it will direct the flow of your conversation. Starting with general questions about an author's early writing and development, as well as influences on their work, allows both the interviewer and the writer to get comfortable with the conversation and warmed up to each other. These early questions help to establish a rapport that can carry you into deeper terrain. As you get more specific and particular in your questions, you're faced again with how best to order them. There are two ways to do this:

- Chronologically by book: in this format you ask all of your questions about each book and progress through the books in chronological order, either backwards or forwards. This works well because you can achieve balance in how much weight you give each title. Usually the most recent title receives the most attention.
- By topic or theme: in this format you ask questions in order by topics that might include the writing process, where ideas come from, character, plot, beginnings, endings, revisions, etc. This works for interviewers who are more topically oriented and less linear in their thinking.

When considering how to organize your questions, go by what feels most natural to you as the interviewer. After your specific questions about the work, you can finish with general questions about what an author is working on now, how teaching impacts her writing, or whatever remains unasked at that point.

Developing a standard final question can provide your interviews with a nice signature; it should reflect the nature and purpose of your interviews. My own signature questions are:

- What are the common problems you see in the work of new writers?
- What would you say to new writers working on their first stories or novel?

These simple questions give the author time to offer final words of advice that often reveal her deepest experiences and struggles, and they make interesting reading for *any* reader, not just new writers.

The last aspect of getting everything in order is to make sure that you don't have too many questions—for an hour-long interview, no more than four pages of questions. Authors often want to know how long the interview will take, and as you conduct more interviews, you'll get a feel for how many questions you can get answered in an hour.

### Step Four: Make Sure You've Covered Everything

Once you've fleshed out your questions and got them in a good working order, make sure that you've asked everything you wanted to. Is there anything critical that you've overlooked or not known how to ask? If so, now is the time to identify those questions and get them down. If you're writing for a specific publication, doublecheck with your editor about anything specific he wanted you to explore. If I'm working with a new editor whom I haven't worked with before, I often send the questions to her so that she can see if there's anything she'd like to add.

If you do your interview and later realize that there's something you forgot, most writers will be happy to answer any additional questions, if they're short. Reviewing your questions thoroughly can help you streamline your work and operate in a more efficient and professional manner.

### Step Five: Get Feedback

Since your questions are the roadmap for your interview, you want them to be as sound as possible. So get feedback. Have one reliable reader, a person you respect and trust, give them a look. This can make a world of difference. Remember that Donna Tartt interview where I came up with a different way of asking her about her ten-year hiatus from the publishing scene? Well, I had asked a trusted friend who was also a diehard Donna Tartt fan to review the questions before I sent them off, and she pointed out Tartt's frustration with questions about the decade between her two novels. Recasting that question made the difference in the interview, because rather than turning Tartt off, I gained her interest. My friend also had other comments that improved the questions and led to a more original and thoughtful piece.

Getting feedback is not an admission of weakness. We can't know everything, and so we go to people who have other perspectives. Go to a friend who's a fan of your author, or ask any respected reader to review your questions before the interview. Nine times out of ten they will have suggestions that will improve your work.

## Composing the Questions: Generative Exercise

When you sit down to compose your questions, you have a world of research to fall back on. Simply *brainstorm* and write down everything that
comes to mind, and then you can flesh the interview out and substantiate
your questions with quotes and references to the author's work.

1. What identity issues inform the writer's work (ethnicity, religious beliefs, sexuality, etc.)?

_____

_____

_____

_____

_____

_____

2. What interests inform the writer's work (travel, sports, history, etc.)?

_____

_____

_____

_____

_____

3. List five aspects of the craft of writing that you would like to discuss
   with this writer.

_____

_____

_____

_____

_____

_____

4. List five aspects of the creative process that you would like to discuss with this writer.

_____

_____

_____

_____

_____

5. List five quotes from this writer's work that illustrate any of these aspects of writing.

_____

_____

_____

_____

_____

6. List two quotes from other writers about writing in general that you would like to bring up with this writer.

_____

_____

_____

_____

_____

_____

7. List one quote from a reviewer regarding this writer that you would like to explore with this writer in person.

_____

_____

_____

_____

_____

_____

8. Are there any difficult questions (about failures, shortcomings, criticisms) you have in mind that may require diplomacy? If so, list them here.

_____

_____

_____

_____

_____

_____

## A Word About Ethics

As an author interviewer, you will no doubt develop your own tastes and values with regard to your purposes and your work. Through this book I hope to help you define those ethics, pointing you toward some questions and creating dialogue about those questions that will help you make decisions about your work. Part of what will help you develop your working ethics will be your reasons for doing interviews. My reasons have evolved over time and now include the wishes to deepen my own creative work, to meet writers I admire, to draw out the best of what an author has to offer, to publish, to meet editors, and most of all to build a literary life. As an emerging fiction writer, I've sought conversations with writers I admire and hope to build professional relationships with over time. I do not find it useful to try to trip someone up, catch them in a stupid remark, or trap them in any way. I've had journalists come to my workshops who shake their heads in adamant disagreement when I say this, as they believe pointing out the weaknesses and shortcomings is a critical part of the task at hand. I think that work that focuses upon revealing a person's shortcomings is not well intentioned and will not expose the best of what a writer, or anyone, for that matter, has to offer. When the work is aimed toward a higher, more mutually beneficial ideal, I find that the interview blossoms and takes on a life of its own, both on the page and in the world. As you move forward into this work, think about the kind of interviewer you would like to be, what you would like to get from your author or other subject, and how you would like your own work to be viewed in the world.

9. Are there any personal questions that you can frame in literary terms? If so, list them here.

_____

_____

_____

_____

_____

_____

10. Is there anything painfully obvious that you would like to ask (in a creative way, of course)? If so, list it here.

_____

_____

_____

_____

_____

_____

### Composing the Questions: Checklist

- ☐ Ask questions about the writing process.
- ☐ Ask questions about external influences on the author's work.
- ☐ Ask questions about specific aspects of craft.
- ☐ Use quotes from the author's work to illustrate your points.
- ☐ Use quotes from other writers on craft to lead into questions.
- ☐ Use quotes from reviewers to lead into questions or explore certain points.
- ☐ Zoom in: ask questions about each of the author's books.
- ☐ Zoom out: ask questions of the body of work.
- ☐ Brainstorm, then come up with an order of questions that makes sense to you.

### Interview Question Dos and Don'ts

**Do . . .**
- Use quotes from other writers and reviewers.
- Use quotes from the author's work to elucidate your question.
- Exercise diplomacy.
- Start general and get more specific.
- Give each area of inquiry appropriate weight.
- Demonstrate expertise while staying out of the limelight.
- Listen!
- Behave in a professional manner.

**Don't . . .**
- Ask the author something you could answer by reading his or her work.
- Ask personal questions about the author's life.
- Ask questions unrelated to his or her work.
- Rely on other interviews, articles, or the press kit for your questions.
- Use the interview to show off your own knowledge.
- Gush, ever!
- Show up late, run out of tape or batteries, or fuss with your tape recorder.

# CHAPTER 3

# Let's Look at the Pros

The best way to learn how to construct complex, thought-provoking questions is to take a look at how other interviewers get their subjects talking. By analyzing the questions other interviewers ask and looking at the responses these questions evoke, we can begin to see how research and careful composition work to create a lively and engaging interview. It's important to remember as you begin to compose your questions that they are for the reader as well as for the author being interviewed, and they need to be interesting and engaging for both.

When analyzing interviews, it's useful to look at the question and break it down to its most basic form by summarizing it in a single sentence. Then you can analyze how the additional components of the questions serve to enhance the final product. Some questions to ask yourself:

- What is this question asking of the author at its most basic level?
- How do the quotes used in the question support it?
- How does other information used in the question support it?

We'll start with an interview from the spring 1999 issue of the arts magazine *Bomb* in which Amy Hempel interviews Alan Warner.* It begins with this biographical note, which I will discuss in a later section.

In Alan Warner's native Scotland, in England, and in Ireland where he now lives, the young novelist is a larger-than-life literary figure, One of the Lads of the new Scottish fiction. A former railway worker, Warner is both a thoughtful and intensely intellectual fellow and a glamorous favorite of the press: as one British reporter put it, " . . . if the literary world has a true pop star, a Keith Richards to Irvine Welsh's Mick Jagger, it has to be the uncompromising, hedonistic, and utterly stylish Alan Warner." Warner's first novel, *Morvern Callar*, was published in 1995 to near-universal acclaim. It is the story of a young supermarket worker in a small port town in Scotland who markets her dead boyfriend's novel as her own and heads for the Mediterranean rave scene with the money. Its existential heroine, its immediacy and hyperreal Scots speech and high-velocity sentences won a Somerset Maugham Award for Warner; the novel was also filmed by the BBC. *The Demented Lands* (1997) followed. It's a moody, singular, visionary haunter. This spring, *The Sopranos* is published by Farrar, Straus, & Giroux in the United

---

*Amy Hempel, *Bomb* (Spring 1999): 24–29.

States. Already a bestseller in England, the novel is a bawdy picaresque, funny and moving; it tracks five members of a convent school's choir (Our Lady of Perpetual Succor, a.k.a. the Virgin Megastore) en route to a competition in Edinburgh. It's a youth-cultural romp with its own dead-on logic: warned of the aging property of smoking, one of the girls says, "Good. We'll get into over 21s nights sooner." Though one of the girls is dying, and another's sexuality is doing a turnabout, they are, to a one, spirited and nasty and *game,* and why not?—around the corner is their future, a small-town life defined by limitation. In the meantime, as a critic for the *London Independent* wrote, *The Sopranos* "takes the stereotype of the wild Highland barbarian, re-genders it, teens it and sets it loose."

The interview was conducted by email between New York City and Dublin. I discussed Hempel's first question in the previous chapter and reprise it here:

**Amy Hempel:** My friend, the poet John Rybicki, has one of my favorite descriptions of what it is like to write. He calls it "lunging at vacancy." How was writing different for you in *The Sopranos* from what it was to sit down and write *Morvern Callar?*

This question, in its most simple form, would read "How was writing your most recent novel different from writing your first novel?" She's asking him if the process gets any easier. But what does she gain by including the quote from John Rybicki? First, the quote "lunging at vacancy" is evocative, in that it describes the desperate nature of the creative process. The quote also gives Warner something to react to while considering the question. In addition, including a quote from another writer places the conversation in the larger dialogue of literature. By using a quote from another writer, Hempel is saying that this is something we writers talk about and struggle with on a regular basis. She's asking Warner for his contribution to this collective dialogue. Without the quote, this question is only about Warner and his experience, rather than about writing in general. Let's look at Warner's response:

**Alan Warner:** "Lunging at the bar" might be a more appropriate description of writing when applied to me. I wrote *Morvern Callar* in 1991 when I was poor and working on the railways, living in a run-down flat in Edinburgh, blah, blah, blah. I remember I used to phone in sick some days. "Flu symptoms" was my byline, and I would just type all night, on a cheap old manual typewriter, listening to James Blood Ulmer, New York's greatest guitarist (some of James's music ended up mentioned in the novel). I couldn't afford Tippex correcting fluid on top of my beer allowance, so I would use two or three coats of Milk of Magnesia. I had no publishing contract in those days and when the third or fourth draft of the manuscript was completed, it sat in a box for two years.

*The Sopranos* was written in 1997/8 in very different conditions: *Morvern Callar* and *These Demented Lands* had been published and I'd been a full-time writer since 1995 in a veritable torrent of Tippex correcting fluid. I had a publishing deal and all that.

However, when I sit down with pen in hand I don't recognize or can't remember any big intellectual or emotional differences between how I felt, THEN, isolated and writing my first novel as an unknown writer and how I felt writing my third one or how I feel today, working on what will be my fourth and fifth ones. For me, the challenges and the isolation always feel the same: the excitement of seeing some words suggesting other, better ones; the discovery of new ideas, plot lines and images through the suggestions of the actual drafts when I reread them and most of all, the conception of the novel you have in your head and the actuality of what it is you produce on that page . . . the distance between my vision and its execution pretty much obsesses me and the thrill when better things come out in the execution than were in your head, is a hard thrill to equal! An old art historian teacher of mine, Pete Smith, called it all The Aesthetic Gulp!!!

Take a minute and think about Warner's response. He answers with a joke, and then he launches into the history of his writing experience and his meager beginnings. We learn a lot about Warner's character and his experiences as a new writer through his ruminations on the physical conditions of writing each novel, as well as the emotional and intellectual conditions. He describes both what's different and what isn't different about writing now.

**AH:** You've said that *The Sopranos* is "a Scottish book, it's about hiding what really is." Can you say more about this?

Here Hempel quotes Warner himself, which shows both the reader and the author being interviewed that she's done her homework by reading other interviews with him and/or articles about him. She's picking up on something he previously mentioned that she wanted to know more about. As you conduct your research and read other interviews and articles by your writer, you may find a few examples of statements or phrases that were mentioned in passing but that you would like to explore further. Make note of these for your interview. This works well because the author can rest assured that he's in the care of someone who's taken the time to consider his work and his intellectual life and has a real interest in engaging him on that level.

**AW:** Just an old-fashioned allegiance to good, traditional Truth. Like most writers I'm very keen on the Truth for my characters, but not always for myself! I don't think the Scottish are any more reserved about their true feelings than anyone else. *The Sopranos* are more truthfully themselves when outside that power matrix of the school/religion; otherwise they must "live a lie" for the sake of an easy life, as we all do, but of course my characters, Fionnula and Orla, are concealing their own, vitally important truths: sexuality and mortality. I admire novelists who, sometimes mercilessly, strip down to the truth, like Jean-Paul Sartre, Juan Carlos Onetti or Walker Percy. We're surrounded by lies, in our relationships, in the media, in the Governments and we tell ourselves lies to get through the day, like "Life is not so bad," or "I'll have enough money till payday," or, "There is a merciful God." Generally just by stripping those lies away you get a hell of a lot of drama. You just need to take a phrase like "collateral damage," which means children with their sexual organs and all their other organs, too, blown right out of them, to remind yourself how powerful the truth is.

The Sopranos are also faced with the post-Thatcherite future. Shows you how wide the effects of 80s Thatcherism spread. These 17-year-old girls live in a town with few opportunities for women, job-wise and, if you have taste, sex-wise; the town is rife with teenage pregnancy and alcohol abuse—in short, any small town in Scotland in the 90s. It's difficult to argue how 80s and 90s liberal intellectual feminism has helped these girls. They have no money. They're not going on to further education so they'll probably never leave the town; it's all still about what guy they end up getting pregnant to. It's not very easy to lie to yourself in the bullring of facts. I think that's why, in a couple of my books, I've been drawn to young women characters. I admire them. They have powerful but unaggressive optimism, a lack of bitterness and usually, a congenital sense of humor.

Warner opens up here about his thoughts on that quote and on revealing "the Truth." Readers learn about his ethics and aesthetics as well as what drives him in his work. Warner also talks about his politics and the difficult truths that people, and his characters, live with in Scotland. This simple question evoked a lengthy response, perhaps because it sprang from a quote by the author himself.

**AH:** Are you sick to death of people asking how you write so convincingly in the voices of young women?

This is an interesting approach; Hempel is actually asking him the over-asked-but-must-be-asked question of how he captures the voices of young women so well. It's often the case that the interviewer simply must ask a certain question, even though it's always asked of a particular author. Whether the need for the question comes from the interviewer's own compulsion or from editorial demands, there's always a way to manage to ask it. I used the example earlier of the Donna Tartt interview where I had to ask about the ten-year span between her two novels. The key is to find an interesting way to rephrase the questions, or re-emphasize it, or simply acknowledge, as Hempel does here, that the question is always asked.

**AW:** Not sick at all. Being asked questions like that is agreeably smoother than working in a supermarket checkout, or going to any job at all, with dread in your heart and only bills in your pocket each and every morning. Or being unemployed. We pampered, arty, successful Scot novelists should remember that. I would hope that the voices of my morally-exhausted MALE Scottish characters in *These Demented Lands,* which DON'T attract so much attention, are equally "convincing."

Warner answers her question, but he doesn't answer the more important question of *how* he writes so convincingly in those voices. He gives a funny remark that indicates how he sees these questions as part of his life as a writer and goes on to say that he hopes all of his characters' voices are convincing. Again, we hear a lot about his politics and how he feels about his position as a writer. We're getting to know a lot about Warner and the world he lives in as a Scottish writer, but if Hempel wanted to know how he achieves those credible voices, she hasn't gotten her answer.

**AH:** You've written about your homeland, but not, it seems, about yourself. Yet your background is certainly compelling—why haven't you gone there on the page? Will you at some time in the future?

Hempel is asking if Warner will at some point write about himself and his own experiences. By asking "why haven't you gone there on the page?" Hempel places this question in the context of literature rather than his personal life. She could ask this question in many ways, such as "What is the role of autobiography in your fiction?" Note that she doesn't ask him specific questions about his personal life but opens the door for him to talk about personal things, should he wish to do so. She acknowledges that he's written about his homeland, and that his background is compelling, which demonstrates her knowledge about and genuine interest in him and his work.

**AW:** Compelling, eh? Doesn't seem like that to me when I do my laundry. I'm working on a long book where the lead character, Simon, is a young railway worker in the Highlands of Scotland: I guess it's all going to be there; but he has a brother and I don't. His father is in fishing, which mine wasn't . . . though there is a fair smattering of Black Magic up in the hills! I've always been suspicious of that Kerouac "cult of the writer" approach. I prefer the more classical novel, Constant, Tolstoy . . . Distance, distance, distance. I distrust that approach: "I'll just change the surnames and send off the manuscript!" I hate to see the life outshining the—often life-redeeming—work and I think wild reputations are used to hype up and support inferior work. I see and hear so many great, inspiring things around me each day, learn so many wonderful stories, I don't know how writers can keep that great stuff OUT of their books and just bore us with the supposed urgency of their straight and strict autobiographical prescriptions. It seems to me a little like, when you start writing about yourself you've run out of ideas. There's always parts of the writer in our characters though; in my case especially Morvern, I think. It's back to this terrible situation where the writer and his/her personality become more famous than their work.

Warner provides an interesting insight into the creative life and the nature of the self—what seems compelling to one can be rather banal to another. This response also offers information about how the writer's life inspires, or doesn't inspire, his work. We get a real sense of Warner's artistic drive and personal beliefs about creativity. Hempel then asks Warner about living in a politically volatile city.

**AH:**  My friend, the South African novelist Lynn Freed, was recently asked to be on a panel with other writers from troubled countries. Lynn thought the title of the panel was "Cultural Outrage," and she told the person who invited her that she didn't feel any cultural outrage—that the situation in South Africa was too complex, etc. Then the man said, No, not cultural outrage, cultural outreach. Alan, you're living now in Dublin; do you have any feelings of cultural outrage or outreach?

This would be a personal question about politics if she hadn't included the quote from Lynn Freed, which again places the question into the larger context of literature by highlighting the fact that many writers live in complicated political environments and that this often influences their work. But by adding the bit about outrage and outreach, the question becomes more specific about particular aspects of his political feelings and more focused than if she'd just asked Warner about living in Dublin.

**AW:**  Well, it's easy for us to bellyache on when we don't live in a country, like Turkey or Nigeria, where fellow writers and journalists are being tortured and imprisoned and executed for what they write. In Algeria some years ago, a professor was shot for refusing to deny his admiration of French literature. I find it impossible to avoid cultural outrage as I look around the Europe of today. There's this fat, dumb and happy hallucination in contemporary Europe, boosted by the millennium amphetamine suppositories, that there is some cultural flowering going on just now. My God! MTV attention spans and sound-bite news reporting are becoming frighteningly monolithic; it's suddenly amazingly easy to be radical, to favor radical "underground" art forms as everything becomes so conservative. Consumerism and the ideas that economic growth and expansionism are God have really taken over. There seem few other values and with genocide back in the former Yugoslavia, and most people indifferent to it, I tend to wonder how far we've really come, since, ah, the Spanish Civil War. Because the Media rules over everyone's consciousness and conscience (e.g. ADVERTISING) . . . the Moral buck has passed to the U.S. and the U.N. and the U this and the U that. That allows us in Europe to Not Give A Fuck anymore . . . hey, YOU GUYS and Hollywood have all the power, it's up to YOU, We don't have any POWER anymore so, if you don't mind, we'll just have ourselves a good time watching cable TV while YOU guys sort out the world. This has led to real decadence and moral cynicism in Europe.

Hempel hit a real nerve here, and Warner takes this opening to talk about his political views of Europe and the state of the world. He picks up on the idea of cultural outrage and shares his views on what he sees happening in the mainstream culture of Europe and beyond. How would his response have been different if she had asked him only about living in Dublin? What does the interview gain from her more substantial question?

**AH:** You were born and raised in Scotland, we nearly met when I was in London a couple of months ago, and now you're living in Dublin. At this point in your life, what do you get from this axis: Scotland, England, Ireland?

Hempel points out three different geographies in Warner's life and asks him to consider how these influences intersect in his work. By starting with an anecdotal introduction to the question, the interviewer provides biographical information about herself—she was in London a couple months ago and nearly met Warner—and about Warner—that he was born and raised in Scotland and currently lives in Dublin.

**AW:** The more axis the merrier, but a main one for me is Spain/Scotland. My wife is Spanish but it's only interesting in so far as it affects the books I'm trying to write. I was in the Highlands till I was 21 so no matter what I write, it's through the eyes of a Scottish Highlander. I'm writing a new novel mainly set in Spain and Europe. That's all I can say really. I don't really like new places, they make me nervous. I still think of traveling and living in places other than my village as romantic adventures. Someone asked me to contribute some travel writing recently and I realized I don't know what travel writing means anymore. It seems a false concept to me. Tea & Sardinia and all that.

Alan Warner talks about the main axis of influence on his work and his point of view as a writer regarding place: "no matter what I write, it's through the eyes of a Scottish Highlander."

**AH:** You're getting a pilot's license? What prompted this, and what will you do with it?
**AW:** I'd keep it in my wallet. My village actually has an airstrip and I have this fatal delusion of when I return home, arriving in style!

Take a minute to consider this question and answer. How does it fit in with the rest of the interview? Do you like it? Would you have included it?

**AH:** I find that most writers' dialogue sounds written, not spoken, but yours is uncannily accurate. Does this have something to do with your love of music, or do you just listen closely?

At its most basic, this question asks Warner how he creates accurate dialogue. By getting more specific and asking if his love of music or his listening skills are to account for this precision, Hempel both demonstrates her knowledge about Warner—his love of music—and passes this valuable information on to the reader. Additionally, she gives Warner ideas to react to when considering his response, which covers voice, dialect, language, and the history of Scottish literature:

**AW:** Spoken language, the real voices and dialects of the regions, has been the important aspect to Scottish literature in the last years. The idea that you could, in *The Sopranos,* have a third-person narrative voice speaking the SAME dialect as the characters is wildly exciting to me and this use of working-class Scottish language has revitalized and energized Scottish literature; I think this access to the spoken language of everyday people in Scotland is what makes English literature seem so gray and formal to us. Everybody speaks like a schoolteacher and working-class characters just go "Oi! Awwright Guv'nor." Of course there is a demographic and political point going on here that literature was hardly being written from the working-class point of view with any authenticity. British novelists were middle-class dealing with a middle-class world often far removed from the daily experience of most folk, and certainly LINGUISTICALLY alien. In my books, I've tried to render weird worlds, but in familiar language, which I think explains some of the popularity of my novels among young people.

Warner raises interesting questions about the role of dialogue and goes on to say that the integrity and truth contained in dialogue is what ultimately draws readers into a narrative. Hempel's next question is more involved:

**AH:** Some of the most eloquent moments in your books come when you render the Scottish landscape: "Time wasn't finished with the world here" (*Morvern Caller*). It made me think of the Canadian poet Anne Michaels, saying in her novel *Fugitive Pieces,* "If one no longer has land but has the memory of land, then one can make a map," and, "It is no metaphor to witness the astonishing fidelity of minerals magnetized, even after hundreds of millions of years, pointing to the magnetic pole, minerals that have never forgotten magma whose cooling off has left them forever desirous. We long for place, but place longs for itself." Does longing fuel your work in large or small part?

This question could have been simply "Does longing fuel your work?" What does Hempel gain by including the first quote? The second quote? The quotes carry the reader into the emotional landscape of longing as it is captured in Warner's work and evoked by Michaels's work. *It's important to remember that the questions are for the reader as well as for the author being interviewed.* Hempel locates both the reader and the author in the emotional space from which her question emerges.

**AW:** I'd like to be drawn, like mercury, back to the mountains and fields of my youth, when they seemed so much bigger and summer nights seemed to come on so much more slowly. I do want to return to live in the area of Oban, and I visit a lot to where I was brought up but I know the end of this voluntary exile will affect my writing. I think it's too soon to go back just now and I don't want to throw the balance on the book I'm working on set there. Maybe the book is too personal and too fragile for me to risk writing it amongst loved landscapes (and loved ones) that have aged. One day, when my work is done, I'll go home.

The lyricism in Hempel's quotes eases Warner into a similar mood of lyric reflection. It also gets him talking about the idea of home and the distance from home an author often requires in order to write any kind of truth.

**AH:** I find all three of your novels extremely evocative, though I have never been to Scotland and my most Scottish experience was having my ears pierced with a kilt pin by a roommate in boarding school. Of course, this means you have tapped into Something Universal, but I'm guessing there was no such big reach at the outset.

Hempel raises an interesting question often entertained by writers and critics: "How does one achieve universality in one's work, and is universality something the writer can aim for or is it achieved by other, less obvious means?" By couching her question in the fact that she identifies with the work in spite of her own lack of experience with all things Scottish, she shares her own experience of the author's work, which serves to draw in both the reader and the author. It also adds credibility to the universality of his work by saying that she experienced it that way, as he acknowledges in his response:

**AW:** I wish I could deny it, but I think, though shamelessly ambitious and presumptuous, I was aiming at that big reach from the start. The idea of making the local universal (and the local which I knew intimately but which I didn't believe could have a valid place in literature) is a central thing in my work for me. When I wrote *Morvern Callar* I felt terribly alone, as if I'd taken my world with me into whatever form of silence I was forced, despair, lethargy, bad art, death . . . the idea I could write a book, using aspects of my Highland community and incidents from my youth and most importantly, using the dialect of my homeland and even my family, seemed almost absurd to me even though I continued to work on the book. Because I came from a small village in an isolated part of Scotland, I rightly or wrongly assumed that place had no literary culture or validity of its own and that I was writing in a void about things that could not possibly interest anyone else, but I don't think that led me to try and universalize the material. Though I bizarrely believed all great writing had to be set in Paris or New York or the American South or, at the very least, a Glasgow housing estate and couldn't possibly originate in my all- too-familiar community, my first novel has its strong sense of Morvern being grounded in a definite community. Though I felt tremendous alienation ABOUT my culture and background. I never for a moment considered, though I'd lived in London and Spain, setting the novel anywhere else. It had to be the way it was though I was filled with woe as I wrote it. I realize now that a novel can spring from any geographical place and this taints me with an unfair suspicion of "metropolitan" novel writing. The London novel, the New York novel of manners . . . etc. . . . tends to get me reaching for writers who seem to write the geographical peripheries: E. Annie Proulx, Knut Hamsun, Cormac McCarthy, Duncan McLean, Juan Carlos Onetti, Peter Handke, Denis Johnson, Joao Guimaraes Rosa, Haldor Laxness, etc.

This question gets Warner talking about central issues for him in his work, and the drive he feels to write his own experience into the language. Many new writers go through the experience of feeling that their own world is not worthy of literature because they've never seen that world reflected there. It's interesting that he didn't believe his background worthy of literature, and yet he was compelled to write from that place regardless.

**AH:** When you spoke of you self-imposed temporary exile from Oban, I thought of something Alice Munro said about the betrayal—that was her word—of leaving home, especially in the working classes. Something about how one begins to talk differently, for example, and feels guilty about it. In fact, one of her books is titled *Who Do You Think You Are?* Does this strike a chord with you? Even though you celebrate the place you came from?

Hempel wants to know if Warner feels guilty about his success, as people from working-class backgrounds often do. The Alice Munro quote brings the conversation into the context of the literary life and gives Warner something substantial to consider about the ways in which one changes and then feels guilty about it. These words spark strong feeling in Warner:

**AW:** There's always an element of cruelty about the interview form which is at the heart of its popularity. Yet I feel a foolish need to be honest. I resent the word "betrayal"—if that's how Alice Munro feels about her past then that's her problem, not mine. My feelings are totally positive. I never betrayed my background at all. "Betrayal" sounds like an excuse for snobbism, as does starting to talk differently. Basically I associate my 21 years in Oban with my Love for my Parents. I've always been deeply uncertain as to my status as a member of the working class and, thankfully, deeply insecure abut my status now as a member of the middle class! I'm terrified of respectability in all its ghastly forms.

I was born when we lived in a rented room (I was conceived in Spain the day Kennedy was shot). My father was ex-army, and NCO, war hero (North Africa and Italy); he and my mother were working-class. Both left school at 14, grew up very poor, little education. Here's something I never tell anyone but I would slip the note from the envelope and, to protect my father's honor, I would correct the spelling mistakes in those sick notes, forging his hand so the teacher wouldn't have one up on my father. You can have a bit of money but not know French or send your kids to piano and ballet lessons or have books in the house: all of which is my definition of being middle class. I was the first member of my family ever (in ALL generations) to go on to Further Education. I still find it inconceivable when I learn someone's father actually went to university.

Yet my father and mother, through the 60s and 70s, owned a respectable/bordering-on-exclusive seaside hotel. We were making some good money in the 70s and my Father knew how to live it up. He drove new Jaguars and I still see him, standing by the dispense with a bottle of Louis Latour 1962 open at his side, grinning at me as another lobster was taken on through to the dining room on an old, banged-up silver platter. That look forced me to be complicit, and said, "Look son, we're ripping off the bastards again." The "bastards" of course were the rich. In 20 years he claimed he'd never met a guest. But we became rich in the 70s. My parents fought badly and when things got bad, one or the other would swish me off . . . the Hilton in Marbella, Churchill's Hotel on Madeira, where sleds speed you down from the mountain top on the cobbles, to outside—the best fish restaurant in town. Playing cards all night on a balcony of the Carlton in Alicante and eating at The Dolphin or billiards against my Father, him reading me *Jaws,* all night long, in his halting words. I had a double upbringing: poor, then there was money, then due to my refusal to conform, poor again. Though I went to university, my jobs on either side of that were all staunchly working-class.

My Dad was a bit of a legend, taught me everything, gent, tough guy and a drinker, hated clever books and learning . . . my relationship with him was real Kafka, Letter-To-His-Father stuff, then in the 80s his drinking got the better of him and I was making no money, I was working in bars, the railways, super-markets, I couldn't function in white-collar jobs; I seemed a son gone astray, so there was an ambience of a fallen family who had once seen better things. I felt a failure as a man and a son and then I had to watch my father die; my books and myself became "successful" immediately after he died and only that made me bitter. I don't feel a single element of betrayal in a class or moral sense, I've always stuck by my guns and I never screwed over anyone to "make a buck." I celebrate and sing my background and if I was half the human being my mother is, I'd be a good person. I spent all my life thinking the world could give me things that were inside me all the time. I think that's the theme of a novel I'm writing.

Warner starts off commenting on the fact that the interview form can get too personal, yet he can't resist the pull of the question or the lure of the form itself. Ask and I will tell, he's saying, when he says: "There's always an element of cruelty about the interview form which is at the heart of its popularity. Yet I feel a foolish need to be honest." He then proceeds to be as honest as one could hope.

**AH:** A number of writers I know feel that a book, as a human document, should be flawed. Are there places where you feel your reach has exceeded your grasp? Something you couldn't get exactly?

This question at its simplest form asks "Where have you failed?" But Hempel poses the question so beautifully by placing it in the larger literary discussion that goes on among writers. The line "A number of writers I know" accomplishes this task succinctly. Rather than talking about failure, Hempel asks if there are places where Warner's reach has exceeded his grasp, a far more diplomatic and less confrontational position to which Warner can respond:

> **AW:** I think every artist hopes to have their best work ahead of them and I pray mine is too. Picasso said a great thing, something like: "To imitate other artists is understandable, but to imitate yourself is pathetic." You have to keep moving on, so I find the work gets MORE challenging and interesting as time goes by and of course, I have dissatisfactions with my published and ongoing work but I also like some of it. All I'm trying to do is learn and become a better writer; to hone my instincts. But I don't think I'd knowingly publish anything that I felt wasn't achieving what I was trying to do. I don't think a book has to be flawed at all. I'd love to write a (in my mind) formally perfect novel that you could read ten years later and not want to change a word. In fact it's my ambition to write the same novel TWICE! (And get the same Advance for it!) So perfect, every word and sentence must be the way it is! Milorad Pavic published *Dictionary of the Khazars* twice, one version with a single paragraph changed!! He called them the Masculine and Feminine versions!!!

How does Hempel's question serve to draw Warner into conversation? What's surprising about his response? What's expected?

> **AH:** There's an amazing scene in *The Sopranos* in which Orla, in a hospital in Glasgow after a visit to Lourdes in hopes of a cure, tries to have it off with a patient in a coma. You navigate expertly between humor and horror and, ultimately, something quite sad in a way that made me think of one of my favorite stories, "Emergency" by Denis Johnson. Do you know it? Is it hard to move between those poles?

What is this question asking at its most basic level? How does the additional information work to create a more evocative question? Break this question down into components and look at how they work together to create a question that ripples beyond the simplistic version: "Is it hard to move between humor and sadness?"

> **AW:** I remember that great Denis Johnson story from his fabulous collection, *Jesus Son*. The character has all those little baby rabbits, cut from a road-kill rabbit, stuffed down his shirt and he's so stoned he sits on them and kills them! Fantastic stuff. I love Johnson's *Resuscitation of a Hanged Man* and *Fiskadoro*. To be compared to Denis Johnson would be a bit too wrong a compliment I

think. I believe the poles you describe are very much those of life itself: beautiful flowers next to dead bodies, etc. Life is pretty horrific, then it's surfeit with beauty also; you cannot deny one or the other. I think the novelist has to take all that on board, and idealism makes for bad novels. I think horrific and humorous events take a big place in the formation of characters' psyches, so it's the perfect excuse to bring it all in.

Warner's response lets the reader know that he's familiar with and admires the Denis Johnson story. He doesn't take the compliment but says that those qualities in his work are taken from life as he sees it. He doesn't take credit for his deft hand in rendering these truths in such a poignant way. Hempel expands upon humor in her next question.

**AH:** In an old interview with Philip Roth, George Plimpton asked if the nightclub act of Lenny Bruce was an influence upon the comic methods Roth used in *Portnoy's Complaint.* Roth said he was "more strongly influenced by a sitdown comic named Franz Kafka and a very funny bit he does called *The Metamorphosis . . .*" Much of *The Sopranos* is very funny, and I wondered who you find really funny, on page or stage.

Hempel's humorous literary anecdote provides Warner with a context in which to address humor. It also provides readers with some background on this question of humor in literature and lets both reader and author know that the interviewer is well prepared for this conversation.

**AW:** I have a real horror of modern "stand up" comedians. I just leave the club and go to a bar when that stuff starts. They strain so much, they're so vulgar and their egos have to be at the center of a joke rather than the formalism of old vaudeville/music hall comedians who have all died out now.

I saw a tape of Jackie Gleason and I think W. C. Fields is hysterical. Laurel & Hardy, who intellectuals have always passed over for colder Chaplin, are so tragic and good. In writing for comedy I love everything by Sam Beckett who is just one of the funniest but most moving writers ever. He is too intellectualized by Herr Professors and his roaring humor is lost; I just howl and howl till I have to leave before the finish of his plays, even the late ones *Roackaby* and *What when?* Once a dear friend of mine and I went to see *Waiting for Godot* in London. We were terribly ripped and 20 minutes into the First Act, Giles stood up and roared "I'm Godot, I'm here, now we can all go to the bar." He was thrown out. Try reading Beckett's *First Love* aloud without cracking up! Another book that makes me nearly vomit with laughter is *Seven Men* by Max Beerbohm. Kennedy Tool's *Confederacy of Dunces* had a big effect on me when I was

16, but all my friends are down on that book these days. I must reread it. Luis Buñuel's moves are terribly funny, especially the divine *Viridiana and Tristana,* with that sardonic, very Spanish humor.

The next question is to satisfy the interviewer's curiosity, and why not? We talk to authors we admire so that we can ask them whatever we want. This specific question works because it points out an unusual term that most American readers probably wonder about as well.

**AH:** When I was in London, my Scottish host taught me what a "Glasgow Kiss" was. I need help with one expression in your second novel: "Hoody Crows"?

**AW:** I hope your friend didn't demonstrate one! A hoody crow is just a large, black female crow. When I was a child I was told a hoody would come down and poke the eyes out of a baby left unattended in a pram.

Warner gives a brief answer that satisfies Hempel's and the reader's curiosity and also conveys how he relates to the term himself.

In the next question Hempel plumbs the depths of literary history by asking if Warner has relatives where Woolf set her famous novel. This is a question about influence, perhaps, and the power of place.

**AH:** Is it true you have relatives from the island of Mull in the Hebrides? Is that where Virginia Woolf set *To the Lighthouse?*

**AW:** Yes. My mother and all my uncles and aunts are from Mull and I spent summers there and feel a bit of a local too. The island has just tragically lost four young men on their way back home to Iona, between islands in a dinghy at night. Uncannily similar to parts of *These Demented Lands,* I'm ashamed to say.

My Woolf scholarship is poor but I'm sure *To the Lighthouse* is set on the island of HOY up in the Orkney islands near where my great friend, the fantastic story writer and Western Swing expert Duncan McClean lives. Around the time of writing *the Sopranos* I was rereading books set over a 24-hour time span . . . *Under the Volcano, Ulysses,* and I reread *Mrs. Dalloway* . . . I found it faintly ridiculous and insulting, trivializing young men's deaths with this upper-class dinner party as if it was some kind of achievement. I never liked Woolf's work . . . give me the vigor and styles of Christina Stead or Henry Handel Richardson any day.

This next question is interesting in that it draws Warner's attention to a pitfall of success for any writer, the tendency to fall back on one's previous successes without taking on new challenges in one's work. While this question could seem insulting—*Are you implying I would slack off?*—she gets away with asking it by slipping in a complimentary observation.

**AH:** There are writers who, after an initial success, take an attitude and let that substitute for work. But I don't see any slacking off in energy or intent here.

**AW:** I don't see why I should rest on any laurels and I haven't lost any hunger at all. I've only been published for three years and I never wanted to only be read by university professors; I want to sell copies of my books because I believe in them. I'm still surprised and delighted to see my books in airports. I hold a silly theory that writers are good for about 10 years before they start to parody their own style, and run out of the inspiration; so I pray I've a little time yet.

Warner responds with his usual vehemence and also reveals his own anxieties about the creative lifespan for any writer.

**AH:** Your notoriety doesn't have a shape yet here in the States, but in the foreign press a cult of personality has grown up around you. They love your outspokenness, your partying, your wicked provocative humor (you told one reporter your new novel "is shite, but it's better than *London Fields*"). My sense is that you don't take this public persona seriously and are able to have a laugh with it. But does it make you self-conscious?

Here Hempel explores the effects of fame on the writer's psyche. She wants to know if the reality of having the eyes of the world focused on a writer inhibits his work or makes him self-conscious in spite of whatever confidence and success he might enjoy. Warner is thoughtful in his response:

**AW:** I once talked for two hours about Scottish literature to a major newspaper. I talked about synthetic language, the influence of MacDiarmid and Tom Leonard on me, my take on Foucault, etc. When the article was published it was titled "The Sexiest Lips in Literature" and somehow there was no intellectual content whatsoever. I was still naive then and assumed newspapers were actually interested in my books rather than just A Story. I did an interview with *The Time*. I took the journalist to a good restaurant. We shared a single bottle of wine and I was polite and lucid. And I picked up the tab for her meal. When the article came out it was headed "He Might Make His Money From Depictions Of Working-Class Misery But Alan Warner Enjoys The Highlife." When you're dealing with human beings like that you tend to get weary and cynical.

Thankfully I can pick and choose my interviews these days and of course there are many serious intellectual magazines where you can talk freely. I remember that interview you mention; there was a better bit when I read to the journalist in the back of a taxi then threw *The Sopranos* out of the window.

Here, we get a nice taste of what the interview process is like for a writer. Forever misquoted and misunderstood, writers can be frustrated and frightened by the interview process. That's why any interviewer taking the time to get to know about the writer and his work will win a friend in the process of producing an interview that actually reflects him accurately.

**AH:** This last is not a question so much as a comment. There is a line near the end of *Morvern Callar* that makes me teary every time I read it. There is a night when Morvern goes from rave to wave—she leaves a night of dancing and drugs in a club on Ibiza and finds an unpeopled spot of beach. She goes for a sensuous swim in the sea, in the dark, and then says, "I hadn't slept for three days so I could know every minute of that happiness that I never even dared dream I had the right."

What do you think of this ending question for her interview? Hempel draws Warner's attention to an emotionally charged and evocative line that would make almost anyone want to read the book. This question could get Warner talking about any number of things, including that character, or why she had that particular experience, but look at his response:

**AW:** In life I think you can only choose happiness or art. If you're not an artist then I hope you're happy. It would be fortune indeed to get both.

It is fascinating that he focuses on his core belief that you can only choose art or happiness. This last line would be a great quote to work into an interview. You could say, "In an interview with Amy Hempel, Scottish novelist Alan Warner said, 'In life I think you can only choose happiness or art. If you're not an artist then I hope you're happy. It would be fortune indeed to get both.' Do you agree?" This idea of choosing art or happiness, and the far-out chance of getting both, is one that comes up again and again for any kind of artist and is always worth pursuing. These lines end the interview on a very compelling note.

# CHAPTER 4

# Time for the Interview

## Conducting the Interview

Now that you have your list of questions in hand—your carefully thought out, well-ordered questions—you're ready for the interview. This is what all your hard work is about, and you can rest assured that you've prepared yourself well for this important conversation. After considering a few practical issues, you'll be on your way.

### How to Present Yourself

Always present yourself as a professional and be respectful of the author's time. Remember that the author has taken time away from writing to talk with you and work on this interview. Here are a few suggestions that will help you make sure that you are respecting the author's time. Some of these suggestions may seem elementary, but you'd be surprised how often interviews can be disrupted by faulty equipment or irrelevant lines of conversation.

- Make sure your recording equipment is in working order and that you know how to operate it.
- Be well prepared.
- Show up on time.
- Don't sidetrack the conversation or waste time.
- Keep your attention on the author and their work.
- Avoid injecting yourself into the interview or getting too personal.

### In Person, Phone, Email

Interviews can be conducted in several ways. Often a writer's location or personal preferences will determine how you do the interview, but it's important to know that each method has its pros and cons.

*An in-person interview* is wonderful in that you have the often rare opportunity to sit across from an admired writer and engage in conversation about her work. While meeting the author in person lends a warmth and conviviality to the interview, an author can sometimes feel nervous in such close proximity to a stranger—you, the interviewer—discussing something as intimate as her work. This is, of course, not always the case, just something to notice.

*The telephone interview* is in some regards the best of both worlds, in that you have the conviviality of a live conversation coupled with a built-in distance that frees the writer up to speak more openly. I've found that authors often answer the phone happily ensconced in their favorite chair with a cup of tea, and because they're in their own environment, they tend to be more relaxed and more open. I enjoy this method of interviewing for just that reason. You're entering on their lives and listening as they answer the door for the Fed Ex man or stir a pot of spaghetti sauce while offering up thoughtful responses to your questions.

*The email interview,* which would appear to be the least "friendly" form, can actually work quite well. It often takes more than one email to accomplish the interview. I suggest sending all of your finished questions to the author so that they can take the time they need to answer well. Then the author returns the questions, with their responses, and you, the interviewer, read through the interview and insert questions raised by the author's responses. In this way you mimic a conversation without actually having a conversation. One of the major distinctions of an email interview is that you don't have to transcribe the interview from tape. While this may seem like a gift from the heavens, it does deny you the benefit of internalizing the author's words, teachings, and actual voice and intonation. (See "Transcribing the Interview" later in this chapter.)

Often a writer will express her preference right off, insisting that she doesn't have time to meet, or that she prefers email. In this case, it's advisable to operate according to the writer's own preferences, as you want her to feel comfortable and relaxed so that you can have an open conversation.

### Equipment and Other Technical Issues

Always record your interview, unless, of course, it's an email interview. There is no way that you will capture a conversation or be able to remain present to a conversation if you're scribbling wildly in a notebook. By taping the interview you can be assured that you will get everything. You can also make eye contact and listen more closely, and when it comes to transcription, you can rewind or fast forward the conversation as you need to.

A microcassette recorder is convenient because you can easily carry it anywhere. It's also easy to use as you're conducting the interview and transcribing it later. A few rules of thumb:

- Check your tape recorder, then check it again, to ensure that it's functional.
- Make sure that you know how to use your tape recorder well before the interview.
- Always bring extra batteries and tape.
- Set a timer or find a way to notify yourself when you've reached the end of the first side of your tape. It's easy to get swept up into a conversation and have the tape stop and miss forty-five minutes of great dialogue.

If you're conducting your interview over the phone, Radio Shack and other retailers sell devices that can intercept the conversation from the phone and record it to tape. A phone recorder records the conversation as clear as bell, and you cannot live without it if you plan on conducting interviews with writers beyond your local area.

Make sure that you're set up and ready to go before you dial the author. You should be able to press play and get right to work without fiddling with your recorder.

These simple and low-cost tools will make your work easier and more rewarding by freeing you up to simply enjoy the conversation for which you've prepared so hard.

### Your Role as Interviewer

As the interviewer, it's your job to ask well-posited questions that will generate thought-provoking dialogue. Once your question has been asked, your job is then to *listen*. Learning to listen and not chime in is more difficult than you might expect. As human beings, we want to connect, to let the other person in the conversation know that we understand what they're saying, that we agree, or that we have a related experience. We want the admired author to know how smart we are, or how cool we are, and so on. This is our humanity at work. The problem with chiming in is that it inevitably cuts off the author's voice, and the author's voice is what we're trying to get onto the page. I have tapes of early interviews I made with authors where I'm listening to an author reveal some truth about a piece of writing, and then my voice cuts in to make a comment because I just couldn't stop myself. Listening to the tape now, I cringe. I'd interrupted the author's flow and cut off the source of running water I'd been digging for.

This is not to say *don't speak*, or *don't comment*. An interview is by its very nature a conversation. But be very aware of letting the author talk to the end of her thought before you offer your comment or question. If you have to scribble it down so that you don't forget, then go ahead. It's very important to remember that the interview is about *the author*, no matter how well you know the person or how much you have to say that will engage her, you need to keep the focus on the author and her work.

*Using Your Road Map*

Your questions will work like a road map to orient and generally direct you in leading the conversation, but don't be wedded to them. Editor David Fenza remarks that one of the major pitfalls of unsuccessful or less interesting interviews is "Too much commitment to one's own list of questions and not enough interest in the answers and where they might lead." Remember that you're free to branch off into different directions and follow the natural paths that your conversation will inevitably take. When you follow a line of inquiry out to its natural end, you can come back to your list of questions and pick up where you left off. Knowing that your list of questions is available to get you back on track can help you relax into the directions your conversation will take and free you up to be fully present in the dialogue.

Sometimes, you'll ask a question and the writer's response will answer several of your questions all at once. In this case, just cross out those questions and continue making your way down the list.

You may find that as you get into the interview and get a feeling for the writer, certain questions may not seem as relevant as they did when you composed them. Go with your gut. If a question doesn't ring any bells, drop it and move on to something more interesting.

## Transcribing the Interview

Let me begin by saying that I transcribe all of my own interviews and find it invaluable. Sometimes the hardest things we do bring the most benefit and offer the most opportunity for growth, such as push-ups. Transcribing an interview, to many, is tantamount to doing sets of push-ups without a break. While transcribing your interview, you will listen to the conversation over and over again, backing up to make sure you got the right words, then listening and typing, then backing up again, until you feel that you could recite the interview in your sleep. While this tedious task may feel unnecessary and perhaps is the type of thing you would hire someone else to do, transcribing the interview yields tremendous benefits. By listening to the author speak and typing up their words, you internalize his voice and his teachings, so that when it's time to edit the interview, you *know* this writer, how he sounds, what he means. You're in touch with his work and his voice enough to feel comfortable making edits and clarifications.

Also, once you've internalized the writer's voice, it's in you like a memory. When I sit down to work on my fiction and I run into a stumbling block, I have the words of many distinguished writers I've interviewed in my head, offering suggestions, sharing experiences, and informing me as I tackle each new challenge. Through the listening and the typing involved in transcription, you can take full advantage of the author as a mentor. By integrating his words and experiences into your own, you've had the benefit of acquiring that writer as a teacher, a rare opportunity. Once you've read all of the author's work, had the conversation, and finally transcribed the tape, that knowledge will live inside you and resurface as you need it.

Also as you're typing the interview, you may notice verbal ticks or uses of slang that you can eliminate as you transcribe. Verbal ticks include the overuse of "like," "really," "actually," "you know," "uh," and so on.

Through the experience of listening and typing you'll also notice common occurrences in the author's language. For instance, in an interview with Andrea Barrett, I noticed that her "real" answer didn't begin until the second sentence of her response. In that case, the first sentence could almost always be deleted. As you become more adept at transcribing, you'll notice things that you'll want to edit, and your editing work will be easier.

# CHAPTER 5

# Refining the Interview

## Editing the Interview

This process poses some interesting questions. Your editing decisions will largely depend upon where you hope to publish your finished piece. For example, *The Writer's Chronicle* prefers an interview that reads as a literary written piece, clean and crisp, not conversational or loose, much in the style of the *Paris Review* interviews. According to David Sherwin, former editor of *The Writer's Chronicle*, "Tone and syntax should be held to a written standard, not a conversational standard. There are many occasions of lax usage that slip into interviews, and it has an effect upon readers—it makes them take the ideas less seriously. Also, the interviewer should feel free to reorganize the interview and to cut and slash, as answers should be as concise as anything you'd find in a solid essay."

While a newspaper may publish a looser, more conversational piece, I encourage interviewers not to slack off or talk down to their audience. Any editor and every reader will appreciate a lean, well-written interview, and I apply Sherwin's comments to every interview I do for any publication.

Notice that Sherwin raises the issue of the question order. With the whole interview laid out, you may find that, in light of the author's responses, the piece would read better if you move things around so that the answers flow well from one question to the next and the whole reads as a cohesive, well-constructed piece.

David Fenza, present editor of *The Writer's Chronicle*, commented on the problems he sees in interviews submitted to the magazine: "Another common problem is that the submitted interview is too faithful to the actual spoken event. The level of diction is low; the rhetoric is clumsy, halting, verbose. Interviews can be edited for the sake of clarity and concision and still remain conversational in tone and lively."

Feel free to maneuver the interview into its best possible shape. *The goal is to create a literary document, not a record of a conversation.*

### Staying True to the Author's Voice

Edit or change the way an author says something only if it is in keeping with the author's voice in the rest of the piece. Having transcribed the interview and typed all of the author's words, you should be in a good position to make minor edits and clarifications without losing the author's actual voice and language.

### Use of Slang or Curse Words

This can be okay if it is not overdone. When editing out slang or curse words, you can leave a taste of these words to indicate the tone, but leaving all of them will only distract readers from the content in your piece. Of course, this is a delicate balance, but you will eventually arrive at your own conclusions. For now, leave a smattering of them for flavor and get rid of the rest.

### Including the Author in Revision

David Fenza says:

> A good literary interview is not faithful to an actual spoken event. The transcript of the actual spoken interview should only serve as a draft of a dialogue that will, eventually, present the writer as completely and succinctly as possible. A good literary interview is improvisational, but it's also revisionary. Writers are creatures who succeed through revision; they are most themselves when they revise; and this should carry over into the interview.

Since an author interview is a literary document rather than a transcription of a conversation, including the author in your process of revision leads to a much more engaging piece. Remember, writers are not public speakers; they formulate beautiful sentences in the solitude of their own studios. In her introduction to *Writers at Work, Eighth Series,* Joyce Carol Oates makes this point:

> In the *Paris Review* volumes you will find no verbatim transcripts, no fumbling, groping, "spontaneous" utterances; no trailing off into baffled silence; no sense that the interviewer is the "active" component, and the interviewed the "passive"; no misstatements the subject dearly wished afterward to delete, but was prevented from doing so by journalistic exigency or malice. (Cynthia Ozick, for instance, for whom conversation is mere "air," insisted upon typing out answers to her interviewer's questions in his presence and afterward amended the manuscript with oral comments that doubled its length; at a later date, she reviewed and revised her oral comments.)

Oates further points out that the interviews in the text are concerned with recording the truth in the best way possible, and that through allowing the writers to contribute to the interview process by revising and considering their answers before publication, we get the best possible text.

So is the form of the interview merely a pretense, when in fact it is more than a conversation—a written text that surpasses the boundaries of a transcription? On the contrary. The interview form provides the context in which serious issues and questions are explored and, through revision and collaboration on the author's part, presented in their most honest manifestation. Oates goes on to say: "We are likely to be most faithful to our convictions when we have had time to contemplate them. 'How do I know what I think until I say it?' is the classic question, to which the writer instinctively adds, 'How do I know what I said until I have revised it?'" It is the very nature of the writer to revise, revise, revise, and so in capturing the writer's nature, we must allow him the space for his methods.

In addition to stylistic concerns, letting writers in on the editing process serves two purposes. First, knowing that he will be able to revise his words puts a writer at ease with the interview process. If, at the beginning of your interview, you let the writer know that he'll have the opportunity to look over your edited piece and offer revisions, he is then freed up to speak openly without worrying about how well articulated or lyrical his words sound in the moment. Second, you simply get a more accurate, honest interview if the writer has had the chance to clarify and tighten his language after considering his responses.

We want to get the best from the author, and letting him participate in the revisions helps us achieve this end. Remember, though, that it's *your* interview. If an author suggests a change that you don't agree with, discuss it and settle on something that works for both of you. In the interview with Andrea Barrett in *Conversations with American Women Writers,* I asked her why she included actual people from history in her novel *The Voyage of the Narwhal.* She replied that she did so to lend a sense of verisimilitude to her historical fiction, which I thought was a wonderfully informative response because it raised the larger question of how an author creates a realistic historical setting in fiction. Later, while editing, Barrett wanted to cut this question because she found her response lackluster. When I shared with her what I got from her response, we agreed to leave it. I chose to include her in this decision, because I wanted her to feel pleased with the interview, as she'd put time into the conversation and the revisions. This is a decision that each interviewer must make for herself.

### Working with the Editor

When your interview has been accepted for publication, your editor may have comments or suggestions. In general, these will have to do with the editorial preferences of the publication (which you know all about because you've been reading it!). Editors may want you to edit your piece down to fit into a shorter word count, or add information about why readers should care about the author, or ask another question of the author. In general, a good editor's comments and requests will improve your interview. Of course, if you vehemently disagree with a comment, you don't have to do it, but then you may be faced with having to decide between publishing with this editor or not. In this case, you need to stand back and weigh the long-term benefits against the short-term aggravation, then make a decision you can live with. There are no easy answers to these kinds of questions, and they're part of being a real writer, so welcome to your literary life!

Working with various editors and exposing yourself to a variety of ethics, preferences, and working styles will broaden your ideas and help you hone your work as you move forward. Developing good working relationships with editors is essential if you want to continue to get assignments from them or have them take your suggestions seriously.

Additionally, if you publish your interviews in journals that also publish creative writing, a relationship with the editor may create interest in your creative work and get you out of the dreaded slush pile. Many of the benefits you will receive from the work of author interviews have to do with building professional relationships and developing a solid foundation for your literary life.

The edits in the example on pages 72 and 73 are straightforward enough. In the response to the first question, I edited out the *really's,* which Elizabeth overuses in conversation. If I'd been further along in my interviewing career, I would have dropped these occurrences of the word *really* as I transcribed, but as I said earlier, the first few interviews I did, I typed up the conversations in their entirety. The second question I deleted altogether because it didn't add to the interview or take it into new territory. During the interview, after such a brief response, the interviewer simply asks the next question on the list. In the response to the third question, I only had to edit one *really.*

## The Author's Biographical Note

One of your last tasks is composing the author's biographical note, which should include at least the following:
- a list of publications
- a list of awards
- teaching affiliations

Some biographical notes will also create the "character" of the writer, or place the interview in the context of the author's latest works. There

**Examples from the Elizabeth McCracken Interview in** *Conversations with American Women Writers**

## MY EDITS

**How about the playwriting, how did that feed into the fiction?**
I still have to remind myself of some of the things I learned in playwriting. There's a lot of practicality to it, which is ~~really~~ good for me. Especially in early drafts, I'm such a self-indulgent writer. I would ~~really~~ write nothing but long lists of things, people saying, "Well, you know what I think . . ." with no action, no dialogue, for pages and pages. One of the things playwriting did for me was ~~really~~ make me think about action, and think about *economy* in a strange way. It's true there's no budget in fiction, and in playwriting you have to think about how many actors something is going to take and limit the characters. I have a real habit of writing too many characters into something, and when I'm revising—this is what's happening to me now—I always have to winnow characters out, and I always think of it in terms of playwriting. You can reassign dialogue and make a piece more dramatic by having fewer characters. Not that that's true for any play, but for me, I tend to spread the emotion between too many characters.

**Did you write** *Here's Your Hat, What's Your Hurry?* **at the Iowa Workshop?**
No, I wrote about four of the stories at the workshop. The rest I wrote at the Provincetown Fine Arts Workcenter. One I wrote in college.

**Where do your short story ideas come from?**
I wish I knew, because I'd love to write some short stories. I haven't for a ~~really~~ long time. I've written one story in the past six years.

*From Sarah Anne Johnson, *Conversations with American Women Writers* (Hanover, N.H.: University Press of New England, 2004), 128–129.

are several styles of biographical note, and depending on where you publish, you will choose a style that compliments the editorial policies of the magazine or journal.

The purpose of the biographical note is to make readers want to read the interview. If the author is particularly well known or currently in the public spotlight this becomes less vital. If, on the other hand, the author is a newer writer, is less well known, or has been out of sight for some time, an enticing biographical note can let readers know why they should read the interview or learn more about this author. It's up to the interviewer to decide how to best accomplish this with the author's biographical note.

## ELIZABETH'S EDITS

**How about the playwriting, how did that feed into the fiction?**
I still have to remind myself of some of the things I learned in playwriting. There's a lot of practicality to it, which is ~~really~~ good for me. ~~E~~ especially in early drafts, I'm such a self-indulgent writer. I would ~~really~~ write nothing but long lists of things, people saying "Well, you know what I think . . . " with no action, no dialogue, for pages and pages. One of the things playwriting did for me was ~~really~~ to make me think about action, and think about economy ~~in a strange way~~. It's true there's no budget in fiction, and in playwriting you have to think about how many actors something is going to take and limit the characters **to stay within your budget.** I have a real habit of writing too many characters into something, and when I'm revising—this is what's happening to me now—I always have to winnow characters out, and I always think of it in terms of playwriting. You can reassign dialogue and make a piece more dramatic by having fewer characters. Not that that's true for any play, but for me, I tend to spread the emotion between too many characters.

**Did you write *Here's Your Hat, What's Your Hurry?* at the Iowa Workshop?**
No, I wrote about four of the stories at the workshop. The rest I wrote at the Provincetown Fine Arts Workcenter. One I wrote in college

**Where do your short story ideas come from?**
I wish I knew, because I'd love to write some short stories. I haven't for a ~~really~~ long time. I've written one story in the past six years.

*The Straightforward Author's Biographical Note*

The straightforward bio lists the author's publications to date, any awards or prizes received, and teaching credentials. Additional information may include where the author lives as well as how the interview was conducted. Take, for example, the bio at the beginning of an Annie Proulx interview that appeared in the *Missouri Review:*

Annie Proulx has published three novels, *Postcards* (1992), *The Shipping News* (1993), and *Accordian Crimes* (1996), and two story collections, *Heart Songs and Other Stories* (1988) and *Close Range: Wyoming Stories* (1999). She received the PEN/Faulkner Award for *Postcards* and the National Book Award and the Pulitzer Prize for *The Shipping News.* She currently lives and writes in Wyoming.

This interview was conducted via correspondence by *The Missouri Review* staff in May 1999. ("An Interview with Annie Proulx," *Missouri Review,* vol. XXII, no. 2 [1999]: 78)

You'll notice that the bio lists her novels first, then her story collections, then her awards. The interviewer chose to say that Proulx lives in Wyoming because that fact is relevant to her work. It's not necessary to specify the method by which the interview was conducted unless the editor specifically requires it.

If you didn't know Annie Proulx, would this biographical note make you want to learn more? If you were savvy to the ways of the literary world, it most likely would, because a PEN/Faulkner Award, the National Book Award, and the Pulitzer Prize would catch your eye. Even if you weren't so savvy to the lives of the literati, you'd know that a Pulitzer Prize is something special. But what if your author doesn't have these glowing recommendations but is nonetheless worthy of a reader's enthusiastic interest? You may want to consider a narrative biographical note, which will give you room to discuss more specifically the merits of an author.

When asked about the author's biographical note, David Fenza, editor of *The Writer's Chronicle,* said:

We prefer just the facts in the narrative introduction—a short note listing the important books and biographical details. What the readers want, we feel, is to hear the writer discuss the insane and sublime business of being a writer. Serious literary readers don't really care where the interview was conducted or what the interviewer's impressions were about the author's house, cat, spouse, or choice of furnishings. We try to address the serious literary reader and leave the celebrity-glamour-worship to other magazines . . . We want to provide our readers with more than wish fulfillment; we want to provide them with ideas that will be useful the next time they open a book to read or open their journals to write.

Here's a sample biographical note from the Ann Patchett interview in *Conversations with American Women Writers* that first appeared in *The Writer's Chronicle.*

Ann Patchett is the author most recently of *Bel Canto,* winner of the PEN/Faulkner Award, the Orange Prize for Fiction, and a National Book Critics Circle Award Finalist. Her other novels include *The Magician's Assistant,* which earned her a Guggenheim Fellowship in 1994; and *Taft,* which won the Janet Heidinger Kafka Prize. Patchett wrote her first novel, *The Patron Saint of Liars,* while a fellow at the Fine Arts Work Center in Provincetown, Massachusetts. This novel was awarded the James A. Michener/Copernicus Award for a book in progress and was a *New York Times* Notable Book of the Year. Patchett has written for many publications, including *New York Times Magazine, Chicago Tribune, Village Voice, GQ, Elle, Gourmet,* and *Vogue.* (Sarah Anne Johnson, *Conversations with American Women Writers* (Hanover, N.H.: University Press of New England, 2004], 167)

Unlike the Proulx bio, which lists titles in category order (novels, story collections, awards), this bio is in order by novel, listing each one and its associated awards. The bio ends with the other publications for which

### Exercise

Analyze the Ann Patchett biographical note. How is it different from the Annie Proulx biographical note? How is it the same? How will it work to create interest in a reader? Does it live up to Fenza's requirements? Which note do you find to be most effective? Why?

Patchett has written, and since these are major magazines, they add to the reader's overall impression of Patchett as a major writer. Here's another example from the Lynn Freed interview in *Conversations* that first appeared in *The Writer's Chronicle.*

Lynn Freed was born in Durban, South Africa. She came to the United States as a graduate student, receiving a Ph.D. in English Literature from Columbia University. She is the author of four novels: *Heart Change, Home Ground, The Bungalow,* and *The Mirror.* Her short stories and essays have appeared in *Harper's, New Yorker, Atlantic Monthly, Story, New York Times,* and *Washington Post,* among others. She is a member of the core faculty of the Bennington Writing Seminars and lives in Sonoma, California. (Johnson, *Conversations,* 77)

In this bio I started with Freed's birthplace and reason for coming to the United States because this information is directly related to the interview. Then we have the usual list of novels, short stories, and teaching affiliations that once again serves to represent Freed as a highly accomplished author.

### The Narrative Author's Biographical Note

In the Amy Hempel interview with Alan Warner we saw an example of the narrative author biographical note (see p. xx). This alternative to the straightforward biographical note not only offers a feel for the author but also indicates the sensibilities of the interviewer, though keeping the latter out of the spotlight.

### Exercise

Analyze the Lynn Freed biographical note. How is it different from the Proulx and Patchett biographical notes? How is it the same? How will it work to create interest in a reader? Why do you think her birthplace is included? Does the bio live up to Fenza's requirements?

It not only informs us about the background of the author—his previous works, awards, and literary and social reputation, as well as the nature of his work—and sets the tone for the interview to come, it also lets us know in no uncertain terms that we are in the hands of an interviewer who knows her subject and who has a literary force of her own that is ferocious enough to take on the author she has just described.

Describing Alan Warner as "a thoughtful and intensely intellectual fellow" on the one hand and "a Keith Richards to Irvine Welsh's Mick Jagger" on the other, Hempel creates the character who will be at the center of her conversation. She's also researched her subject well, as evidenced by her well-placed quotes and the fact that she can summarize his novels with intriguing and engaging descriptions. The enthusiastic drive of her prose—its literary thrust—launches readers full force into the interview. No reader will want to put this piece down.

The following example is from an interview with Donna Tartt that I wrote for *The Writer* (vol. 116, August 2003, 23–24). This magazine prefers a narrative introduction that "sets up" the interview:

Donna Tartt, the author of the international best-seller *The Secret History*—a college-campus set murder mystery that reveals whodunit on the first page—burst onto the literary scene when she was a mere twenty-eight years old and then just as quickly faded from the limelight back into her cocoon of words. For the past ten years her ardent and devoted fans have been waiting for her follow-up novel, but Tartt, determined not to succumb to the pressure faced by first-time authors with a blockbuster hit to crank out another moneymaker, instead took her own sweet time, setting herself new challenges and taking on a time, place, and subject as far from *The Secret History* as one could imagine.

*The Little Friend* is set in the aftermath of a young boy's murder. Robin Dufresnes was found hanging from a tree in the family's backyard. The main character, Robins sister Harriet, is a precocious twelve-year-old obsessed with Houdini, escape artists, and Captain Robert Scott, who led the doomed 1912 expedition to Antarctica—a hero who couldn't escape.

Harriet becomes fanatical about discovering who murdered her brother and exacting revenge. Her exploits take her into dark and primitive aspects of society and bring her face to face with dangerous criminals. In her adventures she risks life and limb, barely avoiding snakebite, drowning, and plummeting to her death in her quest to bring her brother's murderer to justice. And she has plenty of reasons to want justice. Since the murder her mother has become a depressive alcoholic who never leaves her bedroom. Their home has fallen into a state of disrepair. Her father has moved into the city and taken up with another woman, and her sister Alison is afraid of her own shadow. Readers will turn the page, eager to follow Harriet wherever she leads and hoping with her for justice.

*The Little Friend* resembles *The Secret History* in that they lay out the details of a murder in their first pages, though in *The Secret History* we know who committed the murder, and in *The Little Friend* we never find out. While murder is the backdrop of these tales, it is the aftermath of murder, the affect of murder on the

**Exercise**

Analyze the Donna Tartt biographical note. How is it different from the biographical note for Alan Warner? How is it the same? How will it work to create interest in a reader? Which bio do you find most effective? Why? Answering these questions will help you to identify, as an interviewer, the types of biographical notes that you prefer, but remember that you will always have to negotiate between your own tastes and the editor's preferences.

lives of her characters, that interests Tartt. Her concern is not for the sensational but for the undercurrents and secret tides that determine our human fate.

Tartt is a master at mining the emotional and psychic terrain of characters as diverse and idiosyncratic as twelve-year-old Harriet and her sidekick, Healy, to Farish, a coldhearted ex-con running a methamphetamine lab behind his mother's trailer, and his brother Danny, a lost boy with no options other than to work for Farish, only hoping to one day have money enough to break away.

*The Little Friend* is a symphonic performance that takes readers into pool halls and introduces them to snake charmers, drug dealers, preachers, car salesmen, old aunties—an array of characters from the south. It is a journey you won't want to miss. I had the occasion to interview Tartt after the media rush upon the publication of *The Little Friend*.

The first paragraph lets readers know what's so extraordinary about Donna Tartt and her writing life—the fact that she took ten years to write her second novel after her first huge blockbuster at the early age of twenty-eight—and it tells you about the subject of that first hit book. The next two paragraphs summarize her new novel by explaining the exploits and dilemmas of the main character, Harriet. The fourth paragraph compares and contrasts Tartt's handling of the theme of the aftermath of murder in each novel. The fifth paragraph notes Tartt's particular skill in examining diverse characters, and the final paragraph offers a conclusion to the introduction by painting a broad stroke about the recent novel and describing the circumstance of the interview.

Explained in these pithy terms, it seems that there's nothing at all to writing the narrative introduction, but in fact there is. The narrative is a series of components strung together along the thread of the interviewer's particular interests. While writing the introduction, I had none of these analytic thoughts in mind, only an idea of what information I needed to work into the piece and my own inspiration after having read her work and conducted the interview. The drive of the introduction must come from you, the interviewer, as you consider what is most interesting and inspiring about the author and their work.

The next example of a narrative biographical note appeared in *The Paris Review:**

Amy Hempel does not enjoy interviews. She quotes her friend Patty Marx: "I'm not good at small talk, I'm not good at big talk, and medium talk just doesn't come up." Talking about the self is both unseemly and unnerving, she feels, and dissecting her own deliberate process of composition through, in her words, "pointy-headed questions" tends to provoke her exasperation. This makes for an elusive interview. However, over a humid June weekend at her home last year, Hempel behaved as a polite and gracious host who pointed out the sights and chatted about movies, politics, and theories of pet care but nonetheless wanted very much to be doing all of it away from the tape recorder. Talking about writing, in particular, meant noticing how Hempel loves to quote, at length, those friends and writers dearest to her—and how much she prefers their words to her own.

Born in 1951, Hempel grew up in Chicago and Denver before moving at sixteen to California, the inspiration for what would eventually become the extraordinary, unreal setting for her earliest fiction. She spent time in and around San Francisco until, over a two-year span, a series of significant events unfolded: her mother took her own life, her mother's younger sister soon followed, she was injured in two massive auto accidents and, three years later, her best friend—a young woman who became well-known through Hempel's most anthologized story, "In the Cemetery Where Al Jolson Is Buried"—died from leukemia.

In 1975, Hempel moved to New York City, worked through a couple of publishing jobs, then located a nighttime writing class at Columbia with Gordon Lish, a writer and editor at Knopf whose demanding workshops (Tactics of Fiction) became legendary. Their classes together would mark the start of a long professional relationship, resulting in the 1985 publication of her first book, a brilliantly stylized array of short pieces entitled *Reasons to Live.* At a time when short stories were a publishing standard, hers were an immediate success. She wrote for *Vanity Fair* and the *New York Times Magazine.* She taught classes across the country. In 1990, Hempel brought out her second collection, *At the Gates of the Animal Kingdom,* which, in her words, saw her "branching out from grief to fear." Seven years later, confirming a pattern of taking a long time to write short stories, she returned with *Tumble Home,* a book that put her formal considerations—the packed sentence, the mutability of voice, the suggestive and highly condensed moment—to use in the title novella, her longest work to date.

Hempel recently returned to New York City after five years in Bridgehampton, New York; at the time of this interview she was temporarily in Cold Spring, New York, living in an isolated, modern, one-story wooden house near a lake. Around the house were photographs by William Wegman. Moving boxes. In a sunroom facing a corner was a handsome antique library table. On its surface were the following: a ceramic three-headed dog, a Southwestern lamp, a copy of the *Star* tabloid, books by Walter Kirn and Denis Johnson, fragments of dialogue written in longhand on typing paper, letters for writer friends, an empty silver box the size of a pickle, to-do notes, and a beautifully framed photo of Hempel raising a glass of wine with her two brothers, Gardiner and Peter. There in the country, her

*"The Art of Fiction 176: Amy Hempel," *The Paris Review* (Summer 2003): 30. Reprinted by permission of *The Paris Review.* Copyright © 2003 *The Paris Review.*

**Exercise**

Analyze the Amy Hempel biographical note. How is it different from the Warner and Tartt biographical notes? How is it the same? How will it work to create interest in a reader? Which bio do you find to be the most effective? Why?

newly installed DIRECTV wasn't working, and the only alternative, a VCR, was missing a cable.

This last biographical note is interesting in that it charts Hempel's career against the influences in her life that have fueled her work, and in this sense it offers a real biographical portrait. In the first paragraph, the interviewer sets the stage by letting the reader know how much Hempel dislikes the whole interview process. Right away, the reader will be curious to see how the interviewer draws out her elusive subject. In the second paragraph we learn about the life-changing tragedies that shaped Hempel and drove her to the page. The third paragraph lets the reader know about Hempel's beginnings and her relationship with her mentor Gordon Lish, who published her first collection of stories. We also learn what kind of writer Hempel is, taking a long time for a story and working in what might be considered a minimalist tradition. The final paragraph sets up the circumstances of the interview by inviting readers into the room where it is to take place. Note that the interviewer accomplishes this invitation without any authorial intrusion. *The focus is always on the interview subject—Amy Hempel—and never on the interviewer.*

Where some editors might say that the interviewer veered off course is in her description of the sunroom. It offers nothing of substance by way of introducing the author or her work. Remember David Fenza's words: "The readers want . . . to hear the writer discuss the insane and sublime business of being a writer. Serious literary readers don't really care where the interview was conducted or what the interviewer's impressions were about the author's house, cat, spouse, or choice of furnishings."

*The Narrative First-Person Bio*

The third type of biographical introduction offers information about the author but serves more as a narrative introduction to the interview at hand. The introduction is written from the point of view of the interviewer, usually describing the circumstances of the interview, his relationship with the author, and any other related information. Many students intuitively gravitate toward this style of introduction, though it's generally the

**Exercise**

Analyze each of the sample biographical notes above in light of David Fenza's comments. How does each bio hold up to his editorial preferences?

least effective. The intrusion of the interviewer is generally unnecessary and distracts readers from the subject at hand, the author. This impulse in students or new interviewers often arises from the wish to celebrate their proximity to the admired writer rather than from a clear intention as to what would serve the interview.

There are, however, occasions when this style of introduction can be successful. If the interviewer is an author of some merit and has a literary relationship with his interview subject, the introduction can serve as a kind of literary memoir, describing the author interviewed from the perspective of a peer. In this case the introduction works because readers are interested in what one celebrated writer would have to say about another writer. Say, for example, Rick Moody's interview of Philip Roth. Hearing about Roth from Moody's perspective fascinates readers. The "I" of the first-person narrative in that case is an intriguing "I," whereas if an unknown interviewer interviewed Roth, the "I" becomes less compelling.

*Deciding for Yourself*

Only you can decide which method of biographical note works best for your interview. You will have to take into consideration your own preferences and the preferences of the publication you have contracted with or hope will accept your piece. Many times I've written a narrative introduction for an interview in *The Writer* and then, when that interview was published in *Conversations with American Women Writers,* I replaced that narrative introduction with a straightforward biographical note, the form I chose for the interview collection. In making decisions about the biographical note, weigh your long-term goals against your short-term goals and find something that you can live with and that says what it needs to.

### The Interviewer's Biographical Note

The final bit of information you need to include in your interview is your own brief biographical note, in which you can list any relevant previous publications, degrees, and teaching credentials. This note can be the same biographical note you use in your query letter and other printed materials. Here's an example of the biographical note I use for myself:

I'm a nationally recognized author interviewer and fiction writer with an M.F.A. from the Bennington Writing Seminars. My interviews have appeared in AWP's *The Writer's Chronicle*, *The Writer*, and *GlimmerTrain Stories*. My fiction has appeared in *Other Voices* and *George Jr.* was Permissions Editor and Senior Researcher on *Best American Movie Writing 2001*, and I currently teach *The Art of the Author Interview* in the M.F.A. programs at Bennington College and Lesley University. www.sarahannejohnson.com.

Here's an example of a student biographical note in which she maximizes her limited credentials:

I hold an M.F.A. from the Bennington Writing Seminars. My creative nonfiction has appeared in *Northwest Review* and *Oregon Home*, and my interview with Kim Barnes will appear in the January issue of *Northwest Review*. I've taught creative writing at Central Oregon Community College.

### Multitasking: How Many Interviews in the Fire at Once?

For your first few interviews, it's advisable to focus on one at a time until you get comfortable with each phase of the interview process. But, given the life cycle of an author interview—from its beginning through your research and development of questions, the transcription process, editing, and finally the publication of the finished piece—it makes sense to have several interviews in process at once. I'm currently researching two authors, have one set of interview questions ready for a third author, and have a fourth interview accepted for publication.

Only you can decide how much work you're able to take on at one time. When faced with possibilities, remember that quality is preferable over quantity. Figure out how much work you can handle well and don't take on any more than that. It's better to have one good interview published than three mediocre interviews, and you never want to jeopardize your ability to meet a deadline. As an author interviewer, your publications are all you have to show for yourself, so always put the quality of your work before the quantity of your work, as the quality is ultimately what you will be measured on.

# CHAPTER 6

# Publishing the Interview

## Finding the Right Publication

The art of publishing revolves around your ability to match your interview with a suitable publication. Some writers decide where they want to publish first and then create an interview that will meet the editorial specifications of that magazine. Others do the interview they want to do and find a home for it after the fact. Either strategy can work as long as you're realistic about where you're submitting your work.

I can't stress this point enough: it's vitally important to read several issues of any publication to which you're interested in submitting your work. Studying up in advance can save you a lot of time, stress, and postage. Familiarizing yourself with your target publication will help you decide whether your piece is a good match for it and clue you in to any editorial preferences with regard to style, tone, subject, word length, and so on.

### Create Your Submission Hit List

When considering where to submit your interview, make a list of five to ten publications that you feel are a good match for it. As you're making your list, ask yourself the following:

- Do you have any connections at publications that may help you to place your interview?
- Do you expect to get paid for your interview?
- Do you need to see your interview in print, or would you be happy with an on-line publication?
- Does your interview have a specific cultural or other contextual background that would make it particularly appealing to related publications? For example, I had a student seeking publication for an interview with African American poet Tim Seibles. When *The Writer's Chronicle* turned the interview down, I suggested the *African American Review,* a journal that the student was interested in

submitting her own creative work to as well. Her interview was accepted, and now she's building a professional relationship with the same editors who may one day publish her poems.

The publications you put on your list as places where you want to submit your interview should

- publish author interviews of the type you want to pursue in your own work;
- reach the audience you're writing for;
- have the same literary standards you hope to achieve in your own work;
- reflect your interests and concerns as an interviewer.

For example, you wouldn't send a 7,000-word interview to your local paper, nor would you send a 500-word interview with a local author to *The Writer*. Why? Because the editorial specifications of these magazines would mean an immediate rejection. You need to match your work with suitable publications, and the only way to do this is to go out and read them and use your best judgment.

Additionally, you want to find publications that reach the audience for whom you're writing. For example, if you're doing in-depth author interviews that span twenty-five pages and cover issues specific to writers, you're not going to send that to *Pages* or another magazine for readers. You'd want to submit to publications geared toward a serious literary readership, such as the *Paris Review, The Writer's Chronicle,* or one of the hundreds of literary journals around the country that include the *Missouri Review, Michigan Quarterly Review, Santa Monica Review,* and many others.

By submitting your work to publications that reflect the standards you hope to achieve in your own work, you open yourself up to feedback that can help you reach your desired level of interviewing. And finally, your best chance for publication is with a magazine that reflects and supports your own interests. This is true whether you're submitting interviews, stories, poems, or any other kind of serious work.

### Where to Find Publications

There are many places to find lists of publications, magazines, and journals. For a list of literary journals you can look in the back of *Best American Short Stories. The Writers' Market* contains comprehensive lists of all types of publications, including literary journals, literary magazines, commercial magazines, and so on. You can also search Yahoo.com for listings of websites that host author interviews.

*To Multiply Submit or Not to Multiply Submit?*

Once you've created a list of publications to which you'd like to submit your interview, you're faced with the question of whether to submit to one publication at a time, or to multiply submit. First, make sure that the publications on your list accept multiple submissions, and if they don't accept them, don't tempt fate. You'll need to decide if you want to wait to hear back from that magazine or if you want to get your work in front of as many editors as you can all at once. It's advisable to rate your choices. If a publication that you're very interested in building a relationship with doesn't accept multiple submissions, it may be worth it to you to wait to hear back from that editor before submitting to other publications.

When I submitted my first interview to *The Writer's Chronicle,* I didn't submit it anywhere else because I was very interested in those editors' responses and in building a relationship with them. I felt that their editorial standards reflected the kind of author interview I wanted to do, so if they had turned my work down based on quality, I would've taken that to heart and gone back to the drawing board. If they'd turned it down for some other reason, at least I'd begun a correspondence with those editors and they would know my work and hopefully look at future interviews. As it turns out, the interview was accepted, and it was the beginning of a long and productive literary relationship.

Once you start to build relationships with editors, they'll make a point of getting back to you quickly, and you can often suggest further interviews and get an assignment to interview a particular author.

*Offer an Exclusive Look*

Sometimes offering a two- or three-week exclusive look on an exciting interview can help you get an editor's attention and ensure a speedy response. Let's say that you want to submit to a range of publications, but your first choice is a publication that doesn't take multiple submissions. A two-week exclusive can get you a quick response, so you aren't held up too long waiting for the reply before you submit to other publications. I've used this strategy several times successfully, with the exclusive offer capturing the editor's interest.

*Why Query First?*

There are many reasons to query an editor before sending your interview. Most publications require an initial query, as it saves editors the time spent reading through unwanted submissions. A carefully constructed query letter demonstrates your professionalism to the editor right off the bat, so she's more likely to take your work seriously. When you send a completed interview without a query letter, the editor isn't prepared for the submission, and it may sit unread in a slush pile for months.

If you decide to submit without querying, you must include a cover letter that contains the elements of the query, so the editor understands what you are submitting, why you're submitting to her publication, and what your qualifications are. By submitting a formal query or cover letter you gain an editor's professional respect and offer her the opportunity to take your work seriously.

### The Writer's Guidelines

Most magazines and journals post writer's guidelines on their websites or on the inside cover of the publication. Make sure that you follow these guidelines to the letter. They often include details on how to format your submission. They may require a query letter first or accept finished interviews with a formal cover letter that includes the specified information. Make sure you understand the guidelines so that you get your submission right! The writer's guidelines will also let you know if the publication accepts simultaneous submissions. Often it will, as long as you let the editor know that the interview has been multiply submitted.

### Getting the Query Right

After you've looked at several issues of the publication and determined that your work is a good match for it, then you can submit a query letter. Here are a few rules of thumb to help you nail your query the first time:

- Find the editor's full name on the masthead or from the website. Don't rely on old information or the *Writer's Market,* because editors change jobs all the time. You need the most current information.
- Present yourself in a professional manner. Check and doublecheck spelling and grammar.
- Make sure that you have the address right.
- Follow a business-letter format and include the date on your letter.
- Use standard $8\frac{1}{2}'' \times 11''$ paper.
- Single-space paragraphs and double-space between paragraphs.
- If you mail your query, include a self-addressed stamped envelope (SASE) so that the editor can easily reply.
- Don't forget to include your contact information.

Remember that this is a business relationship and that you are a professional. Don't include any unnecessary information.

**Sample Query Letter**

SARAH ANNE JOHNSON
Street
City, State Zip
Phone

Linda Swanson-Davies
GlimmerTrain Stories
Street
City, State Zip
Month Day, Year

Dear Linda Swanson-Davies:

I am writing in the interest of submitting an interview with novelist and short story writer Andrea Barrett.

Barrett received the National Book Award for Fiction for *Ship Fever*. Her other works include *Servants of the Map, Voyage of the Narwhal, The Forms of Water, The Middle Kingdom, Secret Harmonies,* and *Lucid Stars*. She teaches in the M.F.A. Program for Writers at the Warren Wilson College. Barrett was also awarded a MacArthur Fellowship.

This interview focuses on craft and the writing process and addresses Barrett's fascination with science and with characters obsessed with discovery.

I'm a nationally recognized author interviewer and fiction writer with an M.F.A. from the Bennington Writing Seminars. My interviews have appeared in AWP's *The Writer's Chronicle,* and *The Writer,* and *GlimmerTrain Stories* has purchased the rights to excerpt from most of these interviews. I have fiction in the spring/summer issue of *Other Voices*. I was Permissions Editor and Senior Researcher on *Best American Movie Writing 2001,* and I currently work as the Program Coordinator for the YMCA National Writer's Voice program and the Project Consultant for the Sundance Institute Arts Writing Program. You can learn more about me at my website: www.sarahannejohnson.com.

Thank you for taking the time to consider this proposal. I'll look forward to hearing from you soon.

Sincerely,
Sarah Anne Johnson

*Deconstructing the Query Letter*

The query letter you send to an editor is very much like the query letter you send to an author. While the intent of the letter is different, many of the components are the same.

- *The heading* contains your contact information so that the person reading the query can get back to you.
- *The salutation* is the "Dear Linda Swanson-Davies" line of the letter. Never use "To whom it may concern" or "Dear Editor." Always find out the name of the person who will be receiving the letter. It shows respect and professionalism to address them by name. (If you don't know an editor's name, call the publication and ask.)
- *The statement of purpose* is in the first paragraph. State your purpose as succinctly as possible.
- *A bio* of the author reminds the editor of the author's works, awards, and teaching affiliations.
- *The nature of the interview* is described in the next paragraph.
- *The interviewer's biographical note* is in the next to last paragraph. Your biographical note is there to instill confidence in the editor that you are a professional literary character. You may only have an M.F.A. and a single publication, but those still demonstrate a commitment to the work. Your bio should include your previous related publications, related educational experience, such as an M.F.A., related professional experience, and anything else that will help the editor feel comfortable with your experience.

  My education and background: "I'm a nationally recognized author interviewer and fiction writer with an M.F.A. from the Bennington Writing Seminars."

  My publications: "My interviews have appeared in AWP's *The Writer's Chronicle* and *The Writer,* and *GlimmerTrain Stories* has purchased the rights to excerpt from most of these interviews. I have fiction in the spring/summer issue of *Other Voices.*"

  My related job experience: "I was Permissions Editor and Senior Researcher on *Best American Movie Writing 2001,* and I currently work as the Program Coordinator for the YMCA National Writer's Voice program and as Project Consultant for the Sundance Institute Arts Writing Program."

  Other useful information: "You can learn more about me at my website: www.sarahannejohnson.com."
- *The thank you* is the next-to-last element. As a matter of courtesy, you want to thank the editor for her time and consideration.
- The closing salutation is the final element.

*Query Letter Dos and Don'ts*

**Do . . .**

- Make your query letter professional, no more than one page, succinct, and to the point.
- Be sure that you are querying an appropriate publication and have the right address and the editor's name.
- Address your letter to the correct editor and make sure that you spell his or her name correctly. You can find out who to query by consulting the masthead or website, or by calling the publication directly.
- Always include your contact information—name, address, and telephone number—on the letter!

**Don't . . .**

- Mention previous rejections.
- Tell the editor how long and hard you have been working on this article.
- Make mistakes in spelling, grammar, or presentation. Make sure your writing is clear and vivid, as this letter is in itself a writing sample.
- Include anything not directly related to the substance of your query, such as unrelated information about yourself.
- Discuss issues related to acceptance or publication, such as price, copyrights, etc.

*The Fine Art of Patience*

Once you've submitted your first round of queries—whether it's to one publication or more than one—the waiting begins. This is when having a second or third project in the works can keep you from going crazy. There's nothing worse than waiting, and working is often the only remedy for the burden of time. While you're waiting you could be composing questions on a second interview and reading the books for a third. This strategy has helped me keep my mind off the fate of an interview and focus myself on creating more work. If you've done a good interview and followed the suggestions and guidelines laid out in these chapters, your interview will be published—it's only a matter of where and when.

*The Inevitable Rejections*

Finding the right home for your interview can take time. Think of every rejection as providing information. Was the interview turned down due to the quality of the work? If so, what can you do to improve your work the next time around? Or was it turned down because that journal has a backlog of interviews in the queue waiting to be published? One of my students was disheartened when *The Writer's Chronicle* turned down her interview, but she didn't know that their interviews are scheduled all the way into the next academic year. Often an interview will be turned down because the publication has recently published an interview with or essay by the author. *Tin House* turned down an interview that I did with Lynn Freed because they had just published an essay of hers. I sent the interview to *The Writer* and they published it and it eventually made it to the discussion guide in the back of her book *House of Women*.

Rejection does not always mean that your interview is not good enough. It often means that it doesn't meet a publication's needs at that time. Your job in placing the interview is to find the publication that's the best match for you and your work. Rejection is an unavoidable part of the writing life, and if you do good work, there's no reason to let it get you down. Just keep strategizing about where the best place is for you to submit your work, and at some point, you'll get the good news you've been waiting for.

*Working with the Editor*

Once your interview has been accepted, the editor may ask you to make changes to meet specific editorial preferences or clean up language for clarification. As stated earlier, these changes often have to do with the length of the final piece or an emphasis on special areas of interest. Requested changes will rarely alter the substance of your work, because if an editor wasn't pleased with that, he wouldn't have accepted it in the first place. It's up to you to decide what changes you're willing to make. I've had students call me in a frantic state over some detail that an editor wanted to change. In the event that the detail is irrelevant or insubstantial, I advise them to change it. But you always have to weigh your desire to publish with that editor against whatever changes the editor wants to make in your work. If you feel that the changes improve your interview and help you better realize your own intentions, then the answer is easy. However, if you feel that an editor's requests detract from what you're trying to accomplish, you may want to find a new home for your piece.

When *The Writer* accepts one of my interviews, their preferred word length is usually half or less than half of what I do for an author interview. In this case, I cut the interview to best fit their publication and then add the narrative biographical author note that they like to include with their interviews. I agree to this severe cut in length because I can still publish the interview in its entirety in a book such as *Conversations with*

*American Women Writers,* and because I enjoy working with the editors at *The Writer.* The interview gains me exposure and name recognition, which helps with my other literary pursuits. The interview with Sena Jeter Naslund is an example of one that appeared in shorter format in *The Writer* but is included in its full length in *Conversations.*

Once your interview is revised and ready to publish, the magazine will typeset the copy and send you page proofs. Page proofs are copies of the interview as it will appear in the magazine. You'll need to read these closely and make any last-minute changes or corrections right away, because what you see on these pages is what will appear in print. Often the interview subject will want to take a look at these as well. When you've made all of the corrections, sign off on the proofs and return them by the date specified by the publisher.

## Copyright Issues

As far as the copyright goes, most publications buy first serial rights, in print and online, which gives the magazine the right to publish the interview first, and only once. If you sell first serial rights to your interview, ownership of the interview stays with you, and after the interview is published you can then sell it to other publications that accept reprint options (which means that they don't require first-time rights), or to anthologies, or to any other interested buyer. First serial rights also allow you to rework your interview into an author profile or some other format and resell it to another publication, provided that you credit anything that first appeared in the magazine that purchased first serial rights.

Whenever you sell or reprint your interview, you must credit the publication where it first appeared. For instance, I sold the reprint rights to an interview with Lynn Freed that first appeared in *The Writer* to her publisher for inclusion in the *House of Women* reader's discussion guide. I included an acknowledgment that the interview originally appeared in *The Writer.*

Other categories of rights include one-time rights, second serial rights, and the lucrative category of TV and movie rights, though it's highly unlikely that a publication will purchase these rights for an author interview.

# CHAPTER 7

# Keep Your Interview Working

If you want to keep your published interview productive for you, there is follow-up work to be done. This work involves building relationships to help you sustain your creative life and find the support and recognition you need, as well as finding possible additional opportunities for your interview.

## Follow-Up

Since an important part of getting involved with interviewing authors is the building-up of literary community and a literary life, your follow-up is extremely important and rife with the potential for building relationships.
Here's what to do:

- *Stay in touch with the editor who publishes your interview.* Drop the editor notes or emails about any interviews you have coming out, express your interest in interviewing his authors, and so on. Editors like to be kept in the loop so that they can get a first look at anything you're doing.
- *Send copies of the interview to the writer, the publicist, and the writer's editor.* The writer will love seeing an in-depth interview that goes beyond the standard promotional interview, and if you did a standard promotional interview, they'll love to see something that pushes the boundaries of what this format can achieve.

  The publicist will add your interview to the writer's press kit so that it goes out to major media publications around the country. Your gesture will also alert the publicist to your good work, and he may have other writers in his charge whom you would be interested in interviewing. Go ahead and ask.

  By sending the interview to the writer's editor, you're broadening your circle of contacts, so that if and when you shop your own manuscript, editors will recognize your name and you can even ask an agent to submit directly to any editor you think would be right for your work.

- *Network.* Let people know that you're doing interviews and ask for recommendations on who to interview, introductions, etc. Often you can get introduced or referred to authors through friends and other connections. Ask writers you interview for recommendations of other writers to interview. Authors are always pleased to plug their friends, and if you do a good job on their interview, they'll be interested in hooking you up.
- *Read all of the interviews you can get your hands on.* By regularly reading interviews with authors, you can hone in on your own tastes and firmly establish what you like and don't like, what kind of interview you want to do, what kind of authors you want to talk with, and so on. You can also broaden your ideas for questions and notice interesting techniques at work.

### Finding New Uses for Your Interview

Oftentimes you can find new uses for your interview, or new uses will find you. Editors will contact you for reprint rights for anthologies, newsletters, collections of interviews, reader's discussion guides, and so on. You can create your own new material from an interview by repackaging it as an author profile, or web content, or using parts of it for your own newsletter, website, or other printed materials.

#### Reprint Rights

Many times you can sell the reprint rights to your interview, which means you get paid two, or sometimes even three or four, times for a single interview. Often editors will contact you when they read your interview and request the reprint rights. They usually have a standard price that they pay for the second-time use of an interview. The types of publications that purchase reprint rights include the following:

- book discussion guides
- websites: author websites, publisher websites, on-line literary journals, etc.
- newsletters
- anthologies

If you have an interview with an author who recently published a book that will soon be out in paperback, ask the publicist, editor, or author if there will be a book group discussion guide in the paperback. If so, you may be able to sell the reprint rights to your interview for inclusion in the guide.

Oftentimes, websites want to post author interviews and do not require first serial rights. If there are websites that you're interested in, contact the website editor with an official query letter stating your interest in selling reprint rights. Be sure to follow the query letter guidelines outlined in previous chapters.

### The Art of the Author Profile

An author profile is similar to an author interview, but rather than being presented in a question-and-answer format, the profile is written as a narrative about the author and her work. It incorporates quotes and information from a preliminary interview conducted by the journalist writing the profile, as Alfred Kazen discusses in his introduction to *Writers at Work:*

A profile . . . is a sketch; what used to be called a "character"—a personality is quickly built up before our eyes. It is not an intellectual biography, such as a book on a single man seeks to become; it is a close-up, a startlingly informative glance—usually sympathetic, and even when it is not openly so, the coverage becomes a form of sympathy . . . It is not wisdom that we are trying to understand; it is exceptionality—in the case of a writer, his reputations as a writer, his hold on our imagination, means that for us he is like no one else. The interview becomes a way of getting the writer to document this exceptionality himself.

The author profile is a "startlingly informative glance" at a writer and the inner workings of her writing life that at the same time offers biographical information especially as it relates to the author's work. The introduction to the Amy Hempel interview that appeared in the *Paris Review* is an example of biographical information as related to the author's work. This introduction would in fact provide a solid foundation for developing an author profile, if one incorporated quotes and information from the following interview.

THE LEAD. An author profile, like any article, starts with a lead that will pull readers into the piece and set the tone for the profile to come. Take, for example, the lead for an author profile of Donna Tartt called "Murder in Mind: A Profile of Donna Tartt," which appeared in *Poets & Writers:*[*]

Hear the rasp of sharpening knives? That's the sound critics make in anticipation of their ritual sophomore hazing of an author's second book. The reason that it's unusually loud right now (a Benihana samurai chef convention comes to mind) is that Donna Tartt, whose second novel is about to be published by Knopf, has made her critics wait not the standard two, or even the occasional five, but ten whole years to slice into her magnum (truly; it's 555 pages) opus.

This lead accomplishes a lot in a short amount of space. First off, it hooks the reader with strange and haunting imagery that is unusual for a

*Copyright © 2002 Therese Eiben. Originally published in *Poets & Writers,* November/ December 2002, "Murder in Mind: A Profile of Donna Tartt."

profile, but note that the imagery also links to the themes of murder that run throughout Tartt's novels, and throughout the upcoming profile. The lead quickly becomes a joke about the anticipation of hungry critics. The lead goes on to let us know the most unusual fact about Tartt's upcoming release, that is, the time she took to finish it.

Another strategy for leading into your profile is to use a provocative quote from the author, as in this profile of Marge Piercy written for a local newspaper, *The Cape Cod Voice.*

"The world is full of things to write about. It's a matter of having enough time and managing to survive to do it."

Marge Piercy denounces claims that she is prolific. For Piercy, writing in different genres—fiction, nonfiction, and poetry—means that she never has writer's block; if she's stuck in one, she goes to another. And she seems to have a deep well to draw from, having written 16 collections of poetry, 15 books of fiction and three non-fiction, as well as an anthology and a play. ("Marge Piercy Works Once Again with the Distinctive Poetic Pallette," *Cape Cod Voice* [March 27, 2003]: 40)

The quote from Piercy lets readers know that she is a literary force, and the following sentences substantiate that claim by explaining that she writes productively in various genres. The fact that Piercy denies that she is prolific makes her curious to anyone who struggles to write.

THE ANGLE. The angle of an author profile often has to do with the publication. For instance, the angle for the Marge Piercy profile was things that would interest Cape Codders about her work. The angle for an author profile in *Poets & Writers* would be related to the actual writing and the writing life, as the readers of *Poets & Writers* are writers looking for inspiration and validation on their own journeys toward creative success. An author profile for *Pages* or any of the other literary publications geared to readers would explore issues related to themes and topics of particular interest to readers. For instance, a profile of Donna Tartt would explore what went on during the ten years between her first novel and her second, and what draws her to writing about the aftermath of murder.

KEY COMPONENTS OF AN AUTHOR PROFILE. Any author profile, like any author interview, has certain key components that will always be present. It's useful to identify these components, because when faced with the blank page, many writers don't know where to begin. That's where the old adage *start with what you know* comes in handy. If there are certain pieces of information that we know must be present, we can then get into the swing of the narrative, and the words will flow from there.

Any profile will include the names of the author's books, any awards they've received, and their teaching affiliations, just like the biographical introduction to an interview. But rather than having a separate biographical introduction in an author profile, this information is all worked into the article as a seamless whole. Any relevant biographical information should be included as well. For example, knowing about Donna Tartt's career path, the success of *The Secret History*, and her age when she wrote that book are all relevant pieces of biographical information that help to clarify the forces brought to bear on this young writer's work and life.

Additionally, profiles generally include summaries of what the books are about, or something notable about them, so that the reader has a context in which to understand the author. If you're discussing an interesting aspect of craft or theme with the writer, an illustrative quote can let the reader in on the conversation.

Of course, quotes from the author herself are the most interesting, because readers really want to hear it straight from the source. Author quotes provide the access that the reader wants to feel through reading the profile. Lastly, the editor may have special requests for things he would like you to find out about and include in your piece, and these things are generally related to whatever specialty the publication has. In the case of the *Cape Cod Voice*, editor Seth Rolbein wanted me to include information of interest to Cape Codders as well as information on Piercy's involvement with various political issues in her town of Wellfleet.

THE INTERVIEW THAT PRECEDES THE PROFILE. In many respects, the work of composing an author profile picks up where the interview process leaves off. The first job in getting an author profile together is to interview that author, which requires the same steps as an in-depth interview. You have to do your research, compose the questions, then conduct, transcribe, and edit the interview. This interview is then the raw material for the author profile. When I did the profile of Marge Piercy, for example, I went through the interview process as I would for any other author interview, only when the interview.

FINDING THE NARRATIVE. Now that you've been through the conversation and transcribed and edited it, a narrative may begin to emerge, some line of reasoning or method of presentation that you'd like to pursue in your profile. If this narrative thrust hasn't revealed itself to you, then sit down and look through your interview again for clues to the story that you're trying to tell. Often the responses from the author will lead you in a particular direction or start to hint toward a flow for your profile.

Before you even start writing, remember that there are certain elements that you'll want to include:
- the names of the author's books
- awards and teaching affiliations
- relevant biographical information
- information about the books or something notable about them
- quotes from the author's work

- quotes from the author
- the context of the interview, such as the publication of a new book or a local reading by that author
- anything else the editor specifically requests

If the narrative doesn't come easily to you, you can begin to put your information in some kind of order related to the list above. Remember, when you don't know where to start, start with what you know.

WORKING WITH THE EDITOR. Working with the editor on an author profile is no different than working with the editor on an interview. In general, the editor's comments will be aimed at helping you better achieve your intention, and she will often ask for refinements that stress her editorial preferences. Here's an example of feedback I received from Seth Rolbein, the editor of the *Cape Cod Voice,* on an early draft of the Marge Piercy profile:

This absolutely is on the right track in all the important ways, well over the bar. You'll note there is a repeat graph in there and other things to clean up and shorten . . . One notion to consider: I'm not sure if you visited Marge or did this on the phone. If it was in person, and there was a moment, a gesture, a detail, something specific and descriptive that set a tone or defined the conversation or mood, that would be a great way to open this. If not, a strong quote certainly moves in the right direction. . . . Did you mention when the book is appearing in the world, ie a pubdate? I looked quickly but didn't see that.

Seth is a wonderfully supportive editor who knows his trade and often has useful suggestions such as these. Note that there's nothing in his comments that seeks to change my intention regarding the profile, only to hone the piece to a finished product. When you have the opportunity to work with an editor like this, you can learn new techniques and add some chops to your writing. For example, his suggestion to find a "a moment, a gesture, a detail, something specific and descriptive that set a tone or defined the conversation or mood" was intriguing. I wasn't able to use it because I did the interview on the phone, but I've filed it away for future use.

Here is the finished article as it appeared in the *Cape Cod Voice* (vol. 2, no. 23, March 27, 2003], p. 40).

Marge Piercy Works Once Again with this Distinctive Poetic Pallette"

By Sarah Anne Johnson

"The world is full of things to write about. It's a matter of having enough time and managing to survive to do it."

Marge Piercy denounces claims that she is prolific. For Piercy, writing in different genres—fiction, nonfiction, and poetry—means that she never has writer's block; if she's stuck in one, she goes to another. And she seems to have a deep well to draw from, having written 16 collections of poetry, 15 books of fiction and three non-fiction, as well as an anthology and a play.

In *Colors Passing through Us,* Piercy's latest book of poetry, Cape Codders will discover a fresh look at our natural world through the lens of Piercy's lyrical descriptions. Readers will find themselves at home with foxes, coyotes, sandy dunes, and the bay in poems like "Quieting on the Bay" and "Resort Offseason."

In reading through the poignant, sometimes mournful, sometimes funny poems, one is struck by the breadth and depth of Piercy's keen attention, not to mention the sheer volume and variety—over 89 poems written over the last three or four years about what has always been most important to her: the lives of women, Cape Cod, Jewish ritual, intimacy and love, and politics.

While Piercy has a reputation for being a bit cantankerous, she was warm, friendly, funny, feisty, and open to honest discussion in a phone interview March 12, the official publication date of the book's release.

She always writes poetry, regardless of what other project she has going, and she still feels most at home with fiction and poetry. "A lot of the nonfiction I do is a task, such as being asked to write an essay on something. It always feels a little bit like being in school," she says.

There is a strong sense of history running through the poems—past, present, and future contained in a single moment, how lives that come before can inform a single life:

*Every aging woman knows that inside,*
*behind her face, her scrawny neck*
*and puffy cheeks, the same swan*
*girl swims over her reflection:*
*we are all that we once were*
*behind the mirror in that downy cave.*

Is her work autobiographical? Piercy thinks not:

"I don't make much of a distinction when I'm writing poems between my experience and other people's. If they move me, they move me. I feel the others, lives very strongly that I'm writing about—the firefighters, the commuter, the woman who leaves her kids and goes to work. In a sense it doesn't matter. When you're writing a poem it becomes transmuted."

In "Sins of Omission," Piercy describes the fleeting quality of memories, especially memories of the dead, and how only through writing those memories come to life:

*What was bright red now*
*is stained like rust. Only*
*in the knotted prayer of a poem*
*can I make those colors gleam.*

Much of her impulse to write stems from a desire to remember: "The mother of the Muses in Greek mythology is memory. I think that has a lot to do with it, the desire that things not be forgotten, especially for me. I was a working class kid. I come from a family that belongs to the invisible, so the idea of preserving my mother's, my grandmother's, lives is important to me."

To both commemorate and find meaning in the tragic events of 9/11, Piercy composed "No One Came Home," an ode to the victims of the attacks as well as a paean to love and humanity:

*When will we understand what terrorists*
*never believe, that we are all*
*precious in our loving, all tender*
*in our flesh and webbed together?"*

This is typical of the poems in *Colors Passing through Us,* hopefulness and human connection in the face of possible annihilation—the annihilation of terrorist acts, the annihilation of war, the annihilation of the self through rage or forgetting:

*The terror has come home.*
*Will it make us better or worse?*

When asked what she believes, Piercy responds with "Choices," a poem she read recently at an anti-war demonstration in Wellfleet:

*Would you rather have health insurance*
*you can actually afford, or bomb Iraq?*
*Would you rather have enough inspectors*
*to keep your kids from getting poisoned*
*by bad hamburgers, or bomb Iraq?*

*Would you rather breathe clean air*
*and drink water free from pesticides*
*and upriver shit, or bomb Iraq?*

"Does that answer your question?" she asks, a gauntlet thrown down.

"We live in a very grim time, so that the pleasures of intimacy, the pleasures you can find in the natural world, the pleasures you can find in friendship and through trying to be active in history, can all provide hope, but I'm also aware of the difficulties of the present."

Piercy captures the passing of a century, the devastation of 9/11, the loss of her mother, loss of all kinds, and yet there is a thread of hope that comes from her connection with nature, her sense of history, and from remaining politically active:

"I'm not a passive person to whom things happen. If you remain politically active you tend to have a little more hope, because you see if you push enough, things change, things give a bit.

"In Wellfleet, we've been very active against the garbage processing factory that they have planned for us. We've done a lot of work on that. At the moment it seems less likely to happen because of the pressure we've put on. You do see things change if you put enough pressure on. If you organize, if you get out there, you often do have an effect. You keep trying to get your views out. You keep trying to reach other people."

That is reason for both activism and writing. *Colors Passing Through Us* gives cause to celebrate an artist and activist in our midst.

# CHAPTER 8

# Interviewing Other Creative People

## Putting These Principles to Use with Other Artists

The principles outlined in the chapters on interviewing an author easily translate to interviewing any creative person, and the same benefits hold true for the interviewer. What better mentors do aspiring artists and creative people have than the people who are already established in their creative fields? For example, a painter who chooses to interview an established colleague with the goal of publishing the interview in an arts magazine will enjoy the benefits gained from his critical research of the painter's work and a look at how the painter's life has informed his work. The interviewer will benefit from the actual dialogue with the painter and from the process of polishing the interview. Through publishing the interview, the interviewer gains recognition for himself as an artistic and critical presence in the larger arts community. This kind of recognition builds professional credibility that can be of great service when one is trying to sell one's creative work.

One of my students who was a screenwriter wanted to interview professional, established screenwriters, thinking that these were the best people to talk to in order to learn about the craft of writing a script and about the business itself. Other students have been interested in interviewing opera singers, ballet dancers, directors, theater professionals, playwrights, and songwriters. They all realized that the nuts and bolts of conducting an author interview were easily transferable to other art forms.

## Example: *Inside the Actor's Studio*

*Inside the Actors' Studio* with host James Lipton is a wonderful example of an interview for a creative person in another field, in this case, acting. The fact that this weekly television program, shown on Bravo, is filmed in front of acting students studying at the New School in New York City is further testimony to the educational benefits of participating in—reading, watching, listening to—interviews with creative professionals. Lipton's approach to the interview form reflects a similar aesthetic and principles to those discussed in earlier chapters. Lipton takes the actor through a series of questions that generally begin with the actor's early life and path to acting, her early development and influences in her acting, and on to her struggles to achieve her acting goals. Lipton asks the actor questions about each of her movies, or if there are too many movies to explore in a single interview, Lipton chooses key examples that reveal new information or illustrate turning points in the actor's career, or that involve especially successful or interesting roles. This pilgrimage through the actor's past often surprises the actor, who perhaps wasn't expecting to be so thoroughly researched and carefully considered. Lipton's preparation and admiration for the actor's work, as they are demonstrated through his carefully composed questions, lure actors in so that they naturally open up. One of the most wonderful things about those interviews is that you can watch an interview with almost any actor, even someone you don't particularly enjoy, and by the end of the conversation you'll have a new appreciation for that person and their struggles. This glimpse into the artist's humanity is what makes *Inside the Actor's Studio* so compelling to so many, and it also demonstrates what a good interview can accomplish.

So what makes James Lipton so good at drawing out his interview subjects?

He spends two weeks compiling extensive information; after his rigorous research, he composes his questions, handwriting them on hundreds of blue notecards, which have become his signature prop. All of this research means that he's always prepared for whatever direction the conversation with the actor will take, and it enables him to stay one step ahead of his interview subjects. Lipton also demonstrates an impeccable interviewer's role by staying out of the limelight himself. As an accomplished director, choreographer, producer, writer for stage and screen, and published author, Lipton is a force of his own, yet he never asserts this. He asks his question and then sits back and delights in the responses. The interviews are edited to fit the television format, and the actors themselves are not included in this process, which is one way in which this medium differs from a written interview with an author. Actors are accustomed to directors shaping a final product, and they live with that representation of themselves.

The process Lipton uses for interviewing an actor is almost identical to the process outlined in this book for interviewing an author:

- Do the research.
- Compose the questions.
- Conduct the interview.
- Edit the interview.
- Publish, or in this case air on national television, the final product.

**Example: Writer A. M. Homes Interviews Painter Eric Fischl**

In the following interview from *BOMB* magazine, acclaimed author A. M. Homes interviews painter Eric Fischl. *BOMB* has been publishing in-depth interviews between artists about the creative process since 1981. The magazine began when a group of friends who were writers, directors, and artists were having a late-night conversation about their creative lives, and they had the idea that they should start a magazine where they could speak about their work in the same way that they spoke about it amongst themselves. I asked Betsy Sussler, editor in chief at *Bomb,* what she looks for in an interview between creative people:

All of our interviewers are conducted by peers, creators themselves who have an intimate knowledge of the creative process. Therefore, the mulling, slow, meandering conversation where ideas can be drawn out and elaborated upon in later rewrites with the participants and *BOMB* editors has always been our approach. The interviews are conversations, blueprints really, a means for further exploration between the two participants that ultimately strives for a revelation or two, something neither one knew before they began, or only had an inkling of, and then, through the process found a way to express it.

The following interview offers an in-depth example of what can be accomplished when two creative people sit down to talk about their work. You can use the same analytic method we used in looking at Amy Hempel's interview with Alan Warner to gain a deeper understanding of the interview. Ask yourself how these questions would read at their most basic. How do the additional elements in the question serve to inform the piece? How does Homes's experience as a creative person offer her additional insight? She begins with a descriptive introduction:

It was the timing, the deft nearly comic timing that first drew me to the work of Eric Fischl. It was the thing about to happen, the act implied but not illustrated, the menacing relations between family members that made Eric Fischl's paintings disturbing. It was the way in which he forced the viewer to fill in the blanks, to answer the question: What exactly is going on here? In his early work invariably the answer was sex; first sex, illicit sex, weird sex, seeing or touching something you shouldn't, rubbing up against the taboos of familial flesh, interracial relations, etc.; the kind of thing you've considered, but aren't necessarily willing to admit. Yet, in order to read the paintings, one had to participate, to admit at least to oneself that yes, we have noticed. It was that, exactly that, the way Fischl subtly and subversively required the viewers to call upon their own experiences, fantasies, nightmares, that impressed me most.

Now, having moved away from the psychosexual drama of the suburban experience to focus on the figure, Fischl remains a compulsively honest painter, depicting the very parts of ourselves we work so hard to keep hidden. In his nudes the body becomes a landscape, the expression of the life lived, physically and emotionally. He turns paint into folds of flesh, curving, contorted, ever-evolving shapes that contain the person we've become. His unblinking, melancholy celebration of the body and all its apparent faults is incredibly significant given the current climate of erasure—surgical cancellation and correction of the very marks that other cultures celebrate: age, weight, and the like. In an America that has developed an addiction for blotting out physical characteristics—our most basic identity—by embracing what is plastic and preserved, Eric Fischl has produced perhaps the most terrifying body of work to date: a series of nudes where we see that even the nude, the stripped figure, wears a kind of psychological clothing that goes beyond the skin. What's hidden is in the thoughts; and this time the figure, the gesture comes closest to the disconnection of madness.

**A. M. Homes:** In writing, in order to pull a story out you go so far into your mind that when you come out you feel you've traveled through time and that either you've been somewhere incredibly different or that the world has changed. And that's a good day's work, but it's not necessarily a pleasant experience. In painting, where do you go?

**Eric Fischl:** You go into the painting. I mean it's the same thing, I would imagine.

**AH:** Does it hurt?

**EF:** Well, every day there's the technical side of the discipline and there are good days and then bad days where the painting is giving me resistance and I don't know how to paint anymore. But there's also the emotional side of the work, the psychological side where you go in and explore feelings and relationships and memories. Often times you find things you're not ready for and you can't bear that this is in front of you. I assume that's the vulnerability you're talking about. I certainly have times where I walk around in my studio thinking: "I can't paint, I'm not as good as I think I am, I'm certainly not as good as everyone else thinks I am." And I'm freaked. The other side is when you've opened a door and you feel the weight of the responsibility. There's something sacred about paint. You make a pact with the painting, you will be responsible for whatever you're putting on it, what you find out.

One of the advantages of one creative person interviewing another is that Homes can share her own experiences as a way to introduce intimate subjects, such as the personal experience of entering into the work. By sharing her own experience, she gets Fischl to open up about himself. Note that she can get away with bringing in her own work and putting her experience on a par with his because she is a well-established artist.

**AH:** I make a pact with myself that despite how I might frighten myself, I'll keep trying. I'm not going to compromise the work because I'm scared. I think your paintings are scary.

**EF:** What paintings? My paintings?

**AH:** Yeah.

**EF:** If you think things and hear voices, that enters you, it touches you but the image can evaporate in some way that when you actually see it in front of you it becomes terrifying. Your imagination can invent and conflate and interpret. Some of it is from what you've experienced, but a lot of it is from things you've heard, things you're imagining could happen. When I went to more realistic representations . . .

**AH:** How and why did that happen?

**EF:** I wasn't good as an abstract artist. It wasn't fun to paint. A good abstract artist doesn't feel the limitations I felt. Also, I went to representation because I wanted a broader audience. I didn't like the pedantic language the formalist painters used. I wanted people to know what they were looking at whether they liked it or not. And then, of course, in moving to representation came the question, What are you going to represent? I never felt confident talking about anything I didn't know much about. I didn't see my source as being greater than myself, my experience.

In the question above, Homes interrupts Fischl's thoughts on fear and how it relates to his own experience. It's important to pick up on his transition to more realistic representations in his work, but the interview would've been served better if she'd let him finish that thought, then picked up on that interesting point. Whenever the interviewer interrupts the interview subject, something is lost. Learning to listen remains the most critical, and often the most difficult, thing to do in an interview.

**AH:** David Smith said an artist can't create outside his time, outside his own experience. Do you think that's true?

**EF:** I was very nervous about getting specific. You start to think: If I paint what I know, how much do I know? Who cares about the little life I came out of? This is before you realize how big everybody's life is. At first I kept it general, I made everything a noun: The TV, The Chair, The Window . . .

Here she offers a quote from another artist, which brings the conversation into the larger world of art. She also has created an intimate rapport with Fischl, so that he shares his anxieties about what his work would show about him as a person.

**AH:** What would happen if you made it specific?

**EF:** I thought it would become a narrow autobiographical experience, or a narrow class experience, and objects would lose their potential for metaphor. I've always tried to edit the objects in my work so that they'd resonate and not be locked in time. I don't engage the world in a direct way. I need the painting to mediate my relationship to it. I need to have the physical distance of a painting to understand life.

**AH:** I'm thinking about the spareness of objects in your paintings.

**EF:** The objects that surrounded my earlier work were objects that extended perception: the telephone, binoculars, a Walkman, a television ... I have mixed feelings about those objects. You rely heavily on them, and at the same time they're alienating devices. You're actually listening to something that's not there. You decontextualize yourself. You're hearing stuff that's not where you are. TV blends into the room situations and events that don't take place in that room. The other kind of objects that I employ would be exotic ones, like statues, and things from alien cultures.

Now the interviewer begins addressing the specifics of his work, getting him to elaborate on the meaning of his artistic choices. Fischl begins talking about decontextualization in his work, an idea that may help readers view his work through a new lens.

**AH:** Like that one in *Slumber Party,* the figure with many arms.

**EF:** The voodoo doll. I grew up in a house with one of those, and all my friends' houses seemed to have a Japanese scroll, a Kontiki head, something that represented otherness, an exoticism. It is not unlike the way we deal with pets, which is that they connect us to something that we're not, something that remains a mystery. It's a prelinguistic experience. Also, putting these objects in your house decontextualizes them and renders them impotent.

**AH:** By taking them out of their culture.

**EF:** Yes.

**AH:** There are some interesting objects in the room in your new paintings, like the tapestry on the wall.

**EF:** It's the room I stayed in in India, that tapestry was on the wall. The first painting is of a woman crouching, looking away, with a black man standing next to her who is very animated and seems to be trying to affect her in some way. As I was looking at this painting I realized you can't see the two figures at the same time. It was the weirdest experience because they're standing right next to each other. You look at the woman, you get so totally absorbed in her inwardness that you don't even know there's this guy right beside her. Then you look at him and he's so different than she is, so animated, half-hidden, half-exposed that you forget all about her. They don't exist at the same moment. That became interesting for me because it posed a question: Is he real? Is she real? Is he a figment of her imagination, a fantasy, a demon? Because this room has suitcases in it, is she leaving, or has she just arrived? And I began, in that room, to chart the journey. The black guy disappears after that first painting, but his presence is always there. She's crawling across the floor. Is she crawling to him or away from him? The painting is stopped at a moment when she is just beginning to unweight one arm. I didn't know if she was doing it as though she were going to move forward or if she was beginning to retreat. She's looking at something off the canvas, there is a presence outside of the painting.

**AH:** So much of your work has been about the interaction of people, the tension and subtlety of that. And in the new paintings it's so markedly different. The woman is looking outside of the painting, but you get the feeling she's not seeing anything. It's not outside, it's in her head.

**EF:** Totally internal.

Homes does a great job of offering readers a broad survey of Fischl's work by describing what his painting used to be about and what it's about now. Her questions don't just ask about the woman in the painting; she notices this image as it compares to previous work and illustrates a key transition in his focus from interactions between people to solitary figures. Even if the reader is not familiar with the painter's work, this question makes sense because Homes put it in context.

**AH:** Her pose and position become animal-like, primal. Have you seen people who have gone crazy? They squat.

**EF:** Well there's *Diary of a Mad Housewife*. She crawls under the table, totally gives up. And the table becomes a compelling object, speaking of objects as metaphors.

**AH:** The woman is in another state that we can't quite get to. There's no relation between her and the outside world, or us.

**EF:** These new paintings are the scariest paintings I've done. They are the most vulnerable. At my opening I didn't come out of the back room. I didn't invite anyone to my opening. I really surprised myself. I'm confident this is some of the best work I've ever done, but it's also so exposed. Someone described the last painting as the "redemption painting," the one of her all balled up, sort of exploded by light. When I was painting it, I couldn't be sure. On the one hand, I felt that she was being annihilated by the light, and that she was returning to the shape with which she had started. Only now, she's completely alone, without even a fantasy, just herself. The tragic end of something. At the same time, there is something so warm about the light. There is a kind of hope from it, that you will transcend your body. The scene with her crawling across the stone floor became an important part of the characterization of the whole environment, the floor turned into a spider web. And the question is: Is she predator or prey?

**AH:** Is she a victim?

**EF:** I think she's a victim of her own desire.

**AH:** What happened to her?

**EF:** She came to that room looking for something. If she was trying to leave the room, then it was a total failure, because she doesn't get out. And if she came looking for something, then maybe that last painting is redemptive. What she first thought she was looking for wasn't what she finally accepted, which was her aloneness. I'm not saying that this is the only experience one can have, but I know what's in the paintings. Before this series, I had my own reasons for making paintings and other people would find other reasons in them that would actually contradict my reasons. But both were equally valid because there was ambiguity in the work. I don't think there's ambivalence in these because the emotional core is so clear. First of all, they're not funny.

Homes succeeds in engaging Fischl in a deep and intimate exploration of his work and the many meanings and subtexts contained in his paintings. She established a trust with him, perhaps because she too is an artist, but also because her questions demonstrate a depth of understanding about what's present in the paintings. She's done her homework and, more importantly, she's let his paintings affect her in a deep way. Fischl and the reader can see that the paintings have had an impact when she observes that "The woman is in another state that we can't quite get to. There's no relation between her and the outside world, or us."

**AH:** That was another question people had.

**EF:** Did you interview thousands, take a poll before you got here?

**AH:** I like to get lots of points of view.

**EF:** Anyway, in comedy you're always giving up something of yourself. You're always taking something that you feel and care about and parodying it. There comes a point in your life when you have nothing left to give away and you take a stand and say this is what there is. And what there is is usually tragic. You were going to ask me about bodies?

**AH:** The whole question of the male gaze. What does it mean for a male painter to be painting this lonely female nude?

**EF:** What it means to be me, a male, is precisely measured by the work itself. I don't take a generalized view. In that series of paintings I chose a black man because he was equally distant from me and her. There were three "others" involved here, three different kinds of experience: me, a white male; him, a black male; her, a white female. All other to each other, an equilateral triangulation of distance. I managed to project into those differences and see, record, what I imagined.

**AH:** Voyeuristically.

**EF:** They're not passive though, they're not pornography. You have an emotional relationship with the person you're watching. I don't think you're seeing things that she's not feeling. It's not as though she's a tragic character and you have the comfort of knowing her fate. You don't stand outside her. You partici-pate in her feelings. Maybe women do not need to meditate, to construct the other in order to measure the distance as a way of understanding themselves, but I think it's very much a part of the male psyche. We are defined by that which we are not.

**AH:** I can't think of another painter, white or black, who paints black people and white people together, especially nude. You've done that a lot. I'm curious about that.

**EF:** It's sexual. I knew that I was dealing with taboos, and that those taboos carry a tension that needs to be explored, maybe exploded, maybe upheld, I don't know. But I knew I was playing in that terrain.

Homes begins an exploration of this "taboo" aspect of his work, plac-ing black and white nudes together in a painting. This question places his work in the context of other painters by pointing out something he does that other painters don't do. She doesn't ask a specific question, instead mentioning her curiosity to perhaps break into a potentially charged line of questioning as easily as possible. Or, perhaps by mentioning her cu-riosity rather than asking a question, she opens the door for him to talk about this issue in his work through his concerns rather than her own.

**AH:** But white and black seem quite comfortable with each other in a lot of the paintings.

**EF:** In most cases the white person would feel like they don't belong there rather than the black character. The white person is the odd man out.

She's pressing him on the point of tension that he mentions in his pre-vious response. This tension is exactly what she wants to detonate in the conversation, and when she doesn't get the answer she's looking for, the all-out explanation or revelation, she presses harder.

**AH:** But I want to know where their relationship comes from. How do they end up there together?

**EF:** I did a painting that started out as a wedding. I painted quite a lot of it—the ceremony, the bride, the groom—before I thought, I don't like this, there's no interest, why am I doing this? So I moved it to the reception after the wedding, from inside to outside, so I could paint Japanese lanterns, people dancing, night light . . . it would be visually more exciting, theatrical. And the bride was really cutting loose, slugging back a bottle of Jack Daniels and there was a black jazz musician whaling away on the piano. Then that got painted over. The painting ended up being three people around a pool, absolutely calm, late at night, like four o'clock in the morning. A white woman sitting in a butterfly chair with a glass of wine looking off the side of the canvas. Leaning against the chair was a black man in a bathing suit with a glass in his hand looking down at this white kid who is sitting by the side of the pool playing with a wind up toy, a monkey that beats a drum. It's a thinly veiled racial slur. The painting's called *The Brat.* This kid is willfully sitting there because he's jealous of his mother's relationship. The black guy is totally, confidently there and looking at the kid like: deal with it. The wedding is hidden underneath it.

Homes gets the deeper response she's looking for in this last question. Because the material under scrutiny is potentially volatile or tense, she's broached the subject in a sidelong manner rather than dead on. She's therefore able to hone in on Fischl's concerns about the tension in these figures until she's finally able to ask the real question, which is "But I want to know where their relationship comes from. How do they end up there together?" This sequence of questions is a wonderful example of how an interviewer can broach difficult questions or address intensely charged aspects of a piece of creative work without alienating the interview subject or causing him to shut down. What if she'd gone right to the heart of the matter by asking how these black and white characters end up together? How would the conversation have unfolded differently?

**AH:** There seems to be a determination to be completely honest. I don't want to see this, you don't want to see this, but if I don't show it to you I'll be lying. Could you talk about that compulsion towards honesty, despite the fact that it may not be pleasant?

**EF:** My imagination is not about flights of fantasy. It's really a process of discovering who I am, so it's about peeling away and peeling away. It's about meeting something essential. The body poses the biggest question for me. It's a question itself. It's all about needs and desires and union and oneness and aloneness. It's all about the edges and boundaries of the flesh, the needs of the flesh. I'm trying to find out what my relationship to the body is, the comfort and discomfort, the appropriate and the inappropriate. You know what I'm saying?

**AH:** Some. Your paintings exist in a very traditional form, yet they're subversive because they do the things that they're not supposed to do. They show you what you don't really want to see, and in such a way that initially the viewer doesn't necessarily notice it.

**EF:** Part of the compulsion comes from growing up in an environment which was both middle class, which has its own restrictions on character, and alcoholic, which has another set of restrictions. The middle class is always en route. It's not a rest place. It's not a place where you want to stay, it's a place

**Exercise**

Analyze the rest of the interview, keeping in mind what you've read so far. Make your own observations about the interviewer's style and analyze how her questions work to draw her interview subject into an in-depth conversation. Think about the following questions:

- Who is the target audience? Does she succeed in addressing them?
- What aspects of this interview are determined by the magazine format?
- What can you learn from the interviewer, A. M. Homes? What does she do well?
- What does she do that you can incorporate into your own work?
- What do you think she could do better? Do you have questions that weren't answered? Were there areas you would like her to have explored? What techniques have you learned in this book that would improve her interview?
- What are your criteria for a successful interview?

that wants to continue to grow. And so it's horrified by any reminder of where it came from, and envious of things that it has not yet attained. The middle class has this denial built into it. Add to that denial the fear that they will be revealed for what they are, that their ambition would be revealed . . . Then the alcoholic thing was stigmatizing when I was growing up, to the point where you couldn't even acknowledge that it was taking place. It's a world in which you couldn't say things which were painfully obvious. If you live in that state then reality doesn't have much meaning for you. Reality became a passion of mine. I willfully chose to be painfully honest. Initially, my paintings pushed it too far. They wanted to be too painful, too confrontational, but in a way that wasn't authentic. It went past the real content to a sensationalism. A lot of the paintings were melodramatic rather than purely dramatic.

**AH:** The lighting in the new work has become much more heightened, more dramatic.

**EF:** It's become almost theatrical. There's not a major work of art that isn't invested with light. Light is absolutely an essential aspect of painting.

**AH:** How do you paint light? It's ethereal.

**EF:** You don't paint light. You feel light. You paint towards a kind of illumination. It's both a psychic illumination as well as a physical illumination. You feel your way towards it through how color works, your relationship to shadow and to highlight, all of those. Each one's a metaphor. There is such a difference between something that is spotlit and something that is luminous, shade and shadow. Very different states of being. It's about casting something in light too. To be an artist you have to engage an audience. You have to use all these things to pull them in, to seduce them. Light is very seductive because it contains mystery and revelation simultaneously. It's also totally outside modernism because in order to really play around with light you have to get past the flatness that is part of the modernist ethic, surface. Light is not about surface, it's about non-surface.

**AH:** Henry Miller talks in an essay about what would happen if he could turn up the light past the full brightness of day. That's part of what's happening here.

**EF:** I started going to art school when I was living in Phoenix. I was influenced initially by the light in the Southwest because it's a very intense flat light that renders everything in two dimensions. You get this cardboard reality. Everything is hard edged, delineated, stark contrast, dark shadow to bright. A lot of my early work used that kind of light. It was part of my ambition to pull these people into the harsh light of day and say, "This is it." Now I'm definitely looking for a much more complicated, emotional light.

**AH:** You paint a lot of naked people. What is nakedness to you?

**EF:** Nakedness is nakedness. I'm affected by it as well. I'm not above it. I have self-consciousness about my body, not unlike most people. But I wonder why it is that the essential self is the uncomfortable self?

**AH:** Any thoughts on that?

**EF:** (*laughter*) No, I just have a career based on wondering about it. On thinking about it. I don't have any answers.

**AH:** You've taken a lot of photographs. They're very snapshotty and yet they're perfectly like your paintings.

**EF:** I was really surprised when I put this portfolio together by how much they looked like my work. My experience is that I watch, I see things. And when I find myself riveted, before I'm thinking anything, but just fixed, that's when I know that this is something I want and I don't know why. My process of painting is trying to contextualize that.

**AH:** When did you start using photography?

**EF:** In 1980, in St. Tropez. The experience of being there was so overwhelming that I couldn't believe what I was looking at. I had no idea how I felt about it. I was so compelled by what I was seeing, I didn't know whether it was a joke, or whether it was wonderful, or horrifying, or stupid, or everything.

**AH:** What you were seeing being . . .

**EF:** I was seeing people on the beach who were naked, who were behaving in a totally socialized way. So that their body language was social language rather than private language. But they were naked, which was the most private place. And so that contradiction was compelling in and of itself. A lot of the gestures were ones that I could take off the beach and put in a living room, or in a bedroom, or in a car, and they would still be active and not about lounging on the beach, which is a whole other kind of body language.

**AH:** Which is what we do, we're not very good on the beach.

**EF:** No. We don't live on the beach the way the Europeans live on the beach.

**AH:** Speaking of photographs, Sally Mann's work on the parent and child relationship shows something so incredibly intimate which we don't otherwise get to see.

**EF:** She's speaking of the reflections of an adult on childhood from a point of sexual knowledge, and we're talking biblical.

**AH:** A lot of your paintings do that as well.

**EF:** To an artist that's absolutely fertile territory. It makes sense to go there because so much of what we're about comes from there. But if we were on Sally Mann's porch watching her kids play in the sun we would not get a drama out of it the way she pulls it out of the black and white. It's sensibility and vision.

**AH:** In your earlier work, a little boy showed up in various incarnations, and then around the time of the India paintings he disappeared. What happened to him?

**EF:** I haven't been able to go back to him. I mean, he is gone.

**AH:** Why?

**EF:** He grew up. He got past the outrage of a child's psyche when what they're promised and what they're given aren't the same thing. You know what I'm saying, right?

**AH:** Yes, I do.

**EF:** We'd all love to find something that gives us fertile ground and makes us famous that we could do for the rest of our lives and that we'd still be good at doing all the way along. But what happened psychologically and emotionally for me was that the early paintings looked up into the adult world, literally, from the point of view of a child: The planes were tilted, the scale was larger than life. At some point after going through the emotional stuff, reliving, re-experiencing, and expressing that emotional discomfort that was there as a child, it was like clockwork. The plane came down, the gaze became eye level, became a one-to-one relationship, it had nothing to do with becoming happy or those kinds of things.

**AH:** That's good to know. (*laughter*)

**EF:** I just started to see it in a more ambiguous way. An adult can accept that situations can be ambiguous, you can have multiple feelings, multiple relationships to the same thing.

**AH:** You literally left and went to India, producing this entirely other body of work.

**EF:** The India paintings were not as different as people think. They were attached to the same impetus. I left that which I knew, went out into a world in which I didn't know anything, and so all I did was watch. The experience of the India paintings was one in which the audience feels alien, even though they're looking at an alien culture, they are the ones that feel alienated. Yeah, it was a fantastic break. It had a particular life . . . intense.

**AH:** That image from the India paintings of an incredibly large nude adult male, standing on his head—you're working with imagery that's at once archetypal and entirely your own.

**EF:** First of all, I'm attempting to do that in lieu of the absence of myths that united society. We used to explain ourselves to each other through our mythology.

**AH:** Which is also moral.

**EF:** Yeah. I prefer the Greek pantheon which divided the human character into all its parts, made each one a god and projected them out into their world to watch them behave. And the way they behaved was instructional. You could see when Eros became a little too needy or insistent or obsessive, bad shit could happen. Or when somebody became too greedy or too powerful, you understood it because they were all parts of something you knew yourself, you could moderate your own behavior accordingly. You had the ability to judge. Americans don't really focus on their history as part of their myth, except the myth of the individual. So I wanted to find within daily life the things that become mythical. Needs and passions. That's why I focused on the family, the most basic structure. Every matrix combination is in there.

**AH:** And the American dream.

**EF:** I've become much more sympathetic to the mentality of the middle class and to their fright.

**AH:** Why?

**EF:** In a way, it is the most interesting aspect of American life. It's the biggest, filled with ambition; the class of transition that tries so hard to uphold the values of the culture. It's tragic and compelling.

**AH:** I have to tell you an Eric Fischl story. One day I look out the window and on the terrace far across the way is a nude man, gardening. I go and get my camera, thinking I'm seeing an Eric Fischl painting, a nude man in the city, gardening. I crouch down because I don't want it to seem like I'm taking pictures of some nude guy gardening. Then the guy goes into his apartment, gets his binoculars and all of a sudden I'm watching a nude guy, who's watching someone further downtown. Then he starts masturbating. And I'm thinking, charming, this is really charming. Then he turns and looks at me with his binoculars. Caught. I totally freak out, drop to the floor of the apartment and literally crawl away. I felt caught and embarrassed.

**EF:** So listen to this. If this happened on the same day, it would blow my mind. My assistant was working over in the West Village renovating an apartment. They were having lunch, and they looked out the window and saw this nude guy on the roof who eventually saw them. They had binoculars and they were checking it out, and then he got binoculars and he was checking them out. And then he started to masturbate.

**AH:** I think there must be a lot of this.

**EF:** Now which part of that do you think is me? You said the Eric Fischl story . . .

**AH:** You would rarely see a picture of, for lack of a better word, an imperfect person naked. And he was doing it publicly and unselfconsciously. There was this hyper-moment around it, this extra-large frame. And then the binocular part got really weird.

**EF:** Yeah, absolutely. Masturbation would be present but it wouldn't necessarily be a thing I would depict. Because at that point it becomes a different relationship . . . It comes to be about something he wants. There's a revelatory moment before the masturbation happens when you see something that is compelling but out of context. This naked person, private and public, gardening and urban, work together to create this weird context. The metaphor that's there isn't there when he starts to masturbate.

**AH:** What makes it erotic is that he's not doing it, which means you're participating by involving your own sense of what is erotic.

**EF:** Exactly.

**AH:** The most fascinating part is how the viewer chooses to participate. Which also makes them have to take a certain amount of responsibility.

**EF:** You always have to include the audience. One way to understand the relationship between an artist and the audience is to look at tennis. In tennis you have yourself and an opponent. And the opponent is going to give you the most resistance to what you're trying to do. And your effort is going to be to dominate that resistance so that you win. That's the battle. And in a sense, your opponent is your audience, because they're the ones who are going to feel and understand all of the intensity and all of the subtlety of your strokes. They're going to know what it feels like when you ace them or you cram a ball down their throat or you drop shot 'em or you pull 'em wider or you mix up the pace. They're going to be affected by it and react to it.

**AH:** Where are the critics?

**EF:** Critics are like umpires. Referees. They're the ones that try to call the out balls, but in my game of tennis, I don't need referees. You don't write for the audience that sits in the stands. You don't paint for those people. But you know that they're watching, and you hope that they're aficionados of the sport, so that they can also appreciate when you do something with incredible touch, or when you masterfully work your way out of a situation, or change the momentum, that they can perceive that moment the way your opponent does.

**AH:** This is the last question. There is an enormous sense of alienation in your work and yet you seem perfectly fine. Are you? And if you really are okay, how did you get to be okay?

**EF:** (*laughter*) Now we are getting to the part where we swap questions, aren't we?

**AH:** No, but literally . . . you do seem fine.

**EF:** Affable and sociable and . . . I don't see a contradiction in any of that. First of all, what do you mean by alienated? The figures seem alienated?

**AH:** Well there's pain, this last set is in more pain than ever. You're enormously successful, a lot of good has happened, how do you reconcile that pain in there with things on the outside? You're trying to expose yourself each time as much as you possibly can. And then it's this weird moment where you're saying, "I hope you like it."

**EF:** Steve Gionakis gave me the best definition of art: "Art is a desperate attempt to make friends."

**AH:** I think it is. People constantly discuss your work in psychological terms, by the narrative. There is so much storytelling in Freud. Do you read Freud?

**EF:** No. I don't know anything about psychology. To me psychological means full of character, and also that the meaning is unconsciously perceived by an audience. Psychology has replaced religion in the way that it can explain the world and the phenomena of the world, our sense of beauty and our sense of purpose to us. So it would make sense that you would make a narrative out of that psychological setting.

**AH:** Do you think people should attempt to tell the story of your paintings in their own psychological narrative?

**EF:** I like that, because it means they are possessing the work. You want possession. You want somebody to internalize it and interpret it in terms that they understand themselves. It's about them. I seek that. What I try to do is narrow the possibility of interpretation to a certain area so that they're never that far wrong. You don't want to control it so much that they have no room. You want them to participate.

### Example: Interview with Screenwriter Max Adams

This is an interesting example, in that the interview explores not only the craft of writing but screenwriting in particular, as well as the leap from screenwriting to writing a book about screenwriting. Let's go through this conversation and see what there is to learn about interviewing a different kind of creative person.

Max Adams is a working Hollywood screenwriter. Recipient of a Nicholl Fellow-ship in Screenwriting from the Academy of Motion Pictures Arts and Sciences and winner of an Austin Heart of Film Screenwriting Award, Adams's award-winning script *Excess Baggage* was purchased by Columbia Pictures and released in 1997, starring Alicia Silverstone. Since dubbed "Red-Hot Adams" by *Daily Variety*, Adams has worked with Hollywood Pictures, Touchstone Pictures, Universal Pic-tures, Walt Disney Studios, and Tri-Star Pictures on a myriad of projects in de-velopment and is currently attached as writer/director to her film *My Backyard*, being produced by Pop Art Films.

This biographical note is straightforward, listing professional creden-tials that will attract an audience of hopeful screenwriters. The following interview was conducted by phone.*

**How did you yourself get involved in screenwriting, and what made you decide to follow this profession?**

I became involved in screenwriting by accident. I was supposed to be a nov-elist, but a friend of mine took a screenwriting class, and I went along, just sort of to see. I fell in love with screenplays and never looked back. So I still have an uncompleted novel, but I have done several screenplays!

The interviewer begins with a general question about getting started. It allows the interview subject to warm up to the interview and gives readers a point of reference about how she first got interested in writing for the screen.

**What was Max Adams like as a boy? Hobbies, interests?**

Here the interviewer gives the first sign of not having done his home-work. Max Adams is a woman as you might have noticed when you read the interviewer's note about her. Max handles the mistake graciously. Her response doesn't offer substantial information about screenwriting, which is no surprise. The question isn't about either screenwriting or writing the book, nor does it demonstrate any knowledge on the part of the interviewer.

Well, surprise, I was never a boy! I was a girl, much to everyone's chagrin. I was skinny, knock-kneed, tall, sarcastic. As a child I was sarcastic, and my aunt tells a story about when I was three and she was saying something to me. I gave her a haughty glare, and I said, "Please, do not harass me!" That was me as a child. I drew a lot. I made up stories, and drew pictures to go with them. Everyone thought I would ultimately be an artist and do drawing, but what they didn't get was that the pictures were just to tell the story, so it's just as well I fell into film. I rode my bike, I roller-skated, I took ballet. I usually had scuffed knees from falling down. I liked to explore, and I read a lot.

**If you are a struggling screenwriter, would you say your best bet would be to geographically relocate to Hollywood in order to get your career started?**

I would not move to Los Angeles to get my career started. I would write a lot of scripts and work on making contact with producers, so that before I got to Los Angeles, I really had a strong handle on my writing and people knew my name. Los Angeles is a very large, harsh city, with a million people trying to get in the door. Without connections, and without having established some rapport with producers, it doesn't make a difference whether you are in Los Angeles or Iowa—you are still outside the door, knocking to get in. If you are already in Los Angeles, that's a plus, because odds are you will just run into people in the industry socially, but I wouldn't move there just for that. I would try to make connections before moving.

This question addresses how to go about building a career. It engages the interview subject and offers the reader useful insight into the realities of breaking into screenwriting. Asking about relocating is much more relevant than Max's childhood, and the reply will be useful to anyone considering what a career in screenwriting will mean to where they can live. How many people would pick up and move across the country if they didn't have to? It's like saying you have to live in New York City to be a novelist, because most big publishers are located there. It doesn't make any sense.

**Would you say your book is targeted more toward an audience of screenwriters who are just beginning, those that have made a few contacts in the business, or both?**

I would say both. The book covers a broad spectrum of stuff, about six years of my life. Some of it's very basic, things as basic as addressing letters to a person. Don't write "Dear Story Writer" or your letter will just go in the trash. But it also covers being in the entertainment industry, situations that arise that can get you into trouble and how to stay out of them, and how to avoid some of the pitfalls that can happen once you have broken through those doors and start making connections.

I'll give you some examples. In the early days, I took jobs which became problematic. I took one job because I liked the story a great deal and I wasn't considering the setting of the story, which was one house. It was a really hard script to write when you just had six people in one house. Things like that you learn as you go, as you take projects. Another project I took was a rewrite of an adaptation. I was in love with the book, and felt that the script had strayed from the book too far and needed to go back to its origins. Everybody in the meeting appeared to think that was a great idea, and I was hired for the project. But I discovered later, much to my horror, the director had never read the book. The director really liked the script, and when I started putting more book back into the story, he didn't like it. If I had been a more seasoned screenwriter I would have learned to look out for things like that, to say casually, "You've read the book, right?"

There are things like this that come up, that help if you are aware of them in advance and you don't find them out post the fact. A lot of that is in the book as well, which I think would be good for writers who are trying to maintain careers, and not just struggle their way in.

This is a great question because it gets right at the specifics of the material presented in the book. The question tries to hone down the audience for the book, which is of great use to the reader, and it engages the screenwriter in a deep way because Adams gives examples from her own life and career experience that demonstrate the issues she addresses in the book. These examples are useful to readers, but also make good reading, offering a glimpse into the life of the creative professional struggling to build a career.

**Would you consider your book to be more of a tell-all of your time in the trenches or a manual of extensive advice to screenwriters everywhere?**
I would consider it extensive advice to screenwriters everywhere. The basis of the book is advice I have given people. It is all taken from questions people have asked me in email or on electronic bulletin boards. The entire book is actually six years' worth of advice I gave people. People kept telling me that I had written a book, and I said that was great, but I hadn't saved any of it! So people I knew started sending me back advice I had given them that they had saved. And it snowballed and became a hobby. When I had filled up three discs and had to buy a zip drive to hold it all, I realized they were right, there was a book there. So this book is advice I gave other people that they felt was worth saving. I give examples from my experience to demonstrate why I have the opinions I have when I give people advice. So there are many examples of situations I've been in that gave me my opinions. But it's not tales from the trenches.

This question appears to be in response to her previous statements, and it's useful in identifying the nature of the book and how the examples of Adams's experiences serve to advise aspiring screenwriters. Her response offers us a look at how the book came into being, and what kind of a teacher she is, and what kind of advice we can expect from her book. Readers are starting to get a feel for the author/screenwriter through her well-positioned responses.

**_The Screenwriter's Survival Guide_ is your first book. In it, you mention the difficulties that you had in Hollywood getting started and how you were able to make a name for yourself. Were those your deciding factors in why you made the choice to write a book on screenwriting?**

No. The deciding factor to write the book was when I got snowballed by people who thought I should write the book and started receiving all the stuff people had saved. This book would never have been written if it weren't for other people pushing me to do it, and sending me back things I had written to them, advising them. It was also very educational for me because in the process of reading all the things people sent me, it reminded me how hard it really was in the beginning. You forget some of that over time; it gets left behind. If I had sat down to write a book from scratch, there are things I wouldn't have remembered to put into the book. But because the material I was getting sent back from other people spanned six years, it was really like reading a diary, and it really brought home to me just how hard it was in the early days. And that kept me going when the book turned into real work!

Here the interviewer demonstrates his knowledge of Adams's book by asking about something the author mentioned in it, and the question elicits an informative response from the author about how she came to write the book. It's a story that many hopeful writers with information and experience to share can relate to.

**Max, did you have a mentor or anyone that inspired you to become a screenwriter?**

Nobody specifically inspired me to become a screenwriter. Like I said, that was an accident. Unless you could say Frank McAdams, my original screenwriting teacher, who first showed me what a screenplay was. Certainly that was the beginning of my love affair with screenplays. While pursuing screenwriting, I have had mentors. Certainly Kurt Ludke, whom I met at the Austin Heart of Film Festival in 1994, has been a patient and wonderful mentor and given me enormous amounts of good advice. And every time I've taken it I've been glad! Greg Beal, who is the program coordinator for Nicholl Fellowships in Screenwriting, has been a wonderful friend and mentor, from the day I arrived in Los Angeles and couldn't find the mall, to my second week in Los Angeles when I had to find a dentist for an emergency root canal, to just giving me advice on the business and being there as a friend. Gale Ann Hurd, who is on the Board of Directors for Nicholl Fellowships in Screenwriting, has been a good friend and mentor and has also given me wonderful advice in times of crisis, and also made the transition to Los Angeles much, much easier. I showed up in Los Angeles so alone, and the first thing that arrived was a welcome basket from Gale. I never will forget that. It made Los Angeles a lot less scary.

The question about mentorship is a wonderful one for an interview with any creative professional. Everyone has mentors. Nobody develops their craft in isolation, and the mentor relationship can provide a fascinating glance into the spirit of living a creative life.

### How does screenwriting differ from writing a novel?

Well, screenwriting is a medium that deals with movement and time, and those are the medium's strong points. You do not have the ability to convey internal thoughts and monologues in a movie the way you do in a novel. So in a novel, the sum of your strongest attributes in telling a story will be the ability to exercise voice, because voice on the page in the novel is apparent, but voice on the page in the screenplay will never be seen on screen. Novels have past, present, and future tenses, whereas screenplays have only one tense—now, the present. Novels have interior monologues and thoughts expressed on the page, and many extra pages for extra detail and descriptions. Screenplays are much like present tense poetry. When you write them, you must be so direct that someone can't misunderstand your meaning in only a very few words. At the same time, you must be ambiguous enough that you can bring many, many more things than the one thing you are saying in a few words into your reader's head, so that they will carry those images and feelings and emotions throughout the entire filming process to ultimately put them up on the screen. So they are very different. Screenplays are much more similar to plays than they are to novels; but again, you have a large difference between plays and screenplays, because plays are static, as far as setting. With screenplays, the sky is the limit as far as setting. You can move between worlds very easily in a screenplay— you can go from Mars to Earth in the space of a second. And you cannot depend on dialogue to carry a screenplay, whereas stage plays are dialogue-driven.

This is a great question about craft, and it draws out a thorough and thoughtful response about the nature of the novel versus the nature of a screenplay. Notice how substantial questions related to the work encourage the most interesting responses.

**William Goldman once said in an interview that he preferred writing novels, but since he seemed to be so good at screenplays, he figured it was how he'd make a living, even if it wasn't his favorite writing venue. How do you feel about that?**

I think a lot of things that William Goldman says are tongue in cheek. He is a very funny man. And while he may have been serious that he prefers novels, I think the rest of that was a little joke.

This question uses the words of a famous screenwriter and novelist to bring up the point that there are novelists who chose to write screenplays either because they're good at it or because the money's better and more secure. Using the example of Goldman works quite well, but the question seems unfinished. Exactly what is the interviewer asking? Is it a question about settling for your second favorite thing, or about making choices, or about money? As a result of the vague nature of the question, the response becomes about whether Goldman meant what he said or not, and so the question never explores that deeper territory about how writers make decisions about their work.

**Who best to ask to review a prelim draft of a screenplay before you get it polished and ready to submit? Friends? Family members? A former teacher?**

Well now, right now, my managers. Before I had a manager, other writers. I would workshop my material with other writers. I was part of an online writer's workshop on Genie, which is no longer there, but it was a pretty powerful workshop, with some smart, talented writers in it. I ended up a film major in college, and would be in screenwriting courses where we would workshop material with fellow students. I would give scripts to teachers for their opinions, and ultimately I would send screenplays out to producers, and get their opinions (which was the final opinion!). I also entered competitions, and when I started doing well in competitions, I knew that I was getting there.

This is a good procedural question. So many writers in all genres show early work to family or friends, who aren't in a position to provide constructive feedback. The suggestions she makes in her response are useful for any new writer. Finding writing workshops and teachers who can provide useful feedback is critical in every writer's life.

**Is there a great market for screenplays, given the amount of movies and television being cranked out these days, especially with the cable TV boom?**

There is more of a market for television because television is the monster that must be fed every day of every week. Television stations have to put something on the air, or people won't watch them, and then people won't buy advertising space . . . uh-oh! With feature films it is a much smaller market, and recently studios have cut back on the number of movies they are actually developing, which is a big blow for future film writers. At the same time, however, cable networks are expanding and developing more new material. Unfortunately, at the present time, right now, there's a possible strike looming, come May 1. Because of this, there is a panic in the industry, and a movement towards reality programming, which is a dent in the television market for writers, because reality programming does not require writers. But *Survivor* was a huge success, and the networks are trying to duplicate it, looking ahead to a time when writers will be on strike, and they will need shows with new content that are not writer-driven. The repercussions of this will be felt whether or not there is a strike, because reality shows in development will exist regardless, and will cut into shows that are written by writers.

Here is another practical questions about where to put one's energies. Getting an insider's view on this critical question will draw in a reader interested in writing for the screen because it addresses his fears that there will never be enough work or enough room for his work in what appears to be a flooded marketplace.

**Your book classifies itself as "the definitive how-to guide to getting read, sold and produced in Hollywood." Can you reveal to us some of the secrets behind getting noticed as a screenwriter in Hollywood?**

(*laughing*) Well, first, the book doesn't classify itself that way, that was the publicist! That's ad hype! I would never say that about my own work, and it doesn't say so in the book. It might be true though, you never know.

Secrets to breaking in. People in Hollywood work long hours, and assistants go home at around 5 or 6, so when you are cold calling agents and producers (and I'll probably get shot for saying this!) producers and agents will be on the phone in seconds saying, "What did you do?" But if you are cold calling agents and producers and you call after 5 P.M., you are more likely to get them directly, and not fight your way through an assistant. When you call an agent, the kiss of death is to say you are a new writer looking for representation. Those are two big red flags—"new writer," and "looking for representation." You always want to ask an agent if they are looking for new clients. And you don't say you are a new writer, just say you are a writer.

Seriously, try to avoid negative comments about movies in conversations you have with people, because the second you say something off the cuff unpleasant about a movie—maybe not the first time you do it, and maybe not the fifth time you do it, but sooner or later—you will discover the person you are talking to produced that movie. And it's not a good idea to hurt people's feelings when you want to work with them. That's a hugely important subject.

Many people feel intimidated approaching the industry and the people in the industry, and so they approach people with a sort of bluster. They will make comments like, "Well, I know that you don't like this kind of material, but . . ." or "I didn't really like your movie, but . . ." They will avoid saying nice things for fear it will be perceived as (for lack of a better phrase) kissing ass. And they are really ready to say negative things, hoping that if they say them first, the other person won't get the opportunity. It's sort of a "knock yourself first, and then no one else can get a shot in" approach. It's driven by fear, and it's a bad approach because it's negative and it hurts other people's feelings. There is nothing wrong with telling someone you like their work—that's not kissing ass, that's a genuine compliment. So I would say if there is one secret to getting in, it's be nice! Oh, and read the book! (*smile*)

Here the interviewer gets the author to reveal some of the secrets in her book in an effort to offer her readers useful information and keep their interest, and also to let readers know what they can expect from the book so they can decide if they want it. The parenthetical inclusion—"(*laughing*)"—does little to further the depth of the conversation. Notations of this nature are an attempt at being cute, which is never appropriate for a serious interview.

**There are several books on the market right now about screenwriters and about screenwriting itself. How would you say your book is different?**
That is the most difficult question to answer because it almost requires that I say something bad about other people's books to make mine look good. "Oh, my book does what that other book doesn't." And I don't like to do that. I think there are many very good books on the market, and they all bring something valuable to a writer. If you are embarking on this as a career, you are going to need to read more than one book. My book is about marketing yourself, and once you break in, surviving the monster that is Hollywood; knowing the ropes, knowing the ins and outs, knowing the pitfalls to avoid, and knowing ways of operating that work. Because if they worked for me, they will work for you, and if they worked for other people, they will work for you. So, it's a market and stay alive book.

There will be other books that will tell you more about craft and more about skills, and you need to read those. There are fascinating books. William Froug has books out that are interviews with screenwriters that are great reading. There is another book, *Conversations with My Agent* by Rob Long, that I just think is required reading—one, because it's funny, and two, because it perfectly documents a relationship with an agent, and it shows you the world and the relationship in reality terms. It's very funny, because most of this is very funny. Linda Seger has wonderful books out. *How to Make a Good Script Great* is particularly good, and it's about craft and storytelling. Richard Walters has good books out, as does David Trottier. William Goldman's books are always entertaining.

What my book does do is tell the truth from a writer's perspective. Any time you are being told the truth from an agent's perspective or a producer's perspective, it is not coming from someone who has seen it from the writer's side of the desk. Agents especially are nefarious in the advice they give—it sounds good, but it's lies. So don't listen to what agents tell you about breaking in, because they have an agenda! Agents will tell you things like "Don't send your scripts to anybody but agents. I want pristine, unread material." Well, that sounds really good, except then they won't read you without a referral. So it's a Catch-22—if you don't send your material to producers, you will never get a referral to an agent, and agents are dogs about only taking material on referral. They give lots of advice like that, that in reality doesn't work. So maybe that's what the book has going for it. I've been there, I've done that, I've bought the t-shirt! There may be other ways to do things, but at least I can tell you the things that worked or didn't, and I will tell you why.

This question gives the author the opportunity to differentiate her book from the many others on the art of screenwriting. What's more interesting, though, is her response; she doesn't denounce other books but instead offers suggestions on what to read and describes what her book includes specifically—the truth from a writer's perspective. Her response reveals a lot about her character—honest, positive, practical, not self-congratulatory. Even though the question is so simple, it really does its job of getting the interview subject to reveal herself and how she feels about her work.

**Okay, so reality shows are in. But we can only take so much of peering at other people—when will networks figure this out? Or better yet, will networks go broke if they do that, then everyone gets wired and uses webcams to do their own peering?**
Boy, I just can't answer for networks. There are a lot of things we are waiting for networks to figure out, and I just can't predict when, or if, it will happen!

What do you think of this question? Is it useful? Does it teach readers anything about screenwriting?

**Are screenwriters employed on a steady basis, or is it a rush, rush, rush, and then wait for months?**
Ohhhhh, it's more rush, rush, rush, and then wait for months. You get paid pretty well, but you are always looking for your next job, and you don't know when it will come. So when you make that first sale, don't buy a Ferrari! Tele-

vision writers go on staff, and when they are on staff, their employment is steady for 13 weeks, or for however long the network has contracted for episodes of the show. So in the long run, television writers get paid less per project, but more over time, just because they work steadily; whereas feature writers get paid more per project, but work fewer projects in general. Unless you are like Aaron Sorkin, who probably works every day of the year!

Another practical question about living the life of the screenwriter yields critical information about bridging the gap between gigs and negotiating down time. All of this will be very important to any reader considering a career in this creative field.

**Are there certain truths that are universal to all good screenplays?**
Yes, there are! They are all written by incredibly talented people, at least initially. And they all address, on some level, the human condition. When writers write, I believe that they write because they have a perspective on the world that is worth seeing, because in some way or other, watching their perspectives and their stories gives our life more depth. They can be simple comedies or great big dramas, but something in the stories in really great screenplays examines the human condition and gives us something to take away with us after we have seen the movie. I think of it as truth through fiction. The stories are made up, but the truths within the stories are universal and world-encompassing. They unite us, the audience, in an exploration of our world.

This series of questions on craft is very good. He addresses an audience of screenwriters and the very real concerns they have about how to go about their creative work. Adams's knowledge and perceptions offer unique insights, and that, after all, is why people read interviews with creative professionals. They want a look behind the curtain at how the magic happens, so they can understand the work they've taken on.

**Do screenwriters fraternize? Do you ever have drinks with Stephen J. Cannell, or talk shop with William Goldman? *grin***
You know, that's a good question. Screenwriters in Hollywood are not encouraged to fraternize. It is actually sort of discouraged, because when writers get together, we can gang up on people and tell tales. Tell each other what we are getting paid. And tell secrets out of school. Combined and united, writers would be a very scary proposition for networks and studios to control! So that's not really encouraged. Writers go out with producers a lot for lunches and meetings. Writers meet with agents a lot for meetings, and certainly talk to their agents a lot on the telephone. But it isn't often you hear someone say, "Hey, I know this writer that you should get together with." So when we do

fraternize, it's either in secret, or it's public and a political statement! (*laughing*) Which is not to say writers don't meet and become friends, but I know an awful lot more producers and studio executives and agents than I know fellow writers.

The use of "*grin*" is unnecessary. In the arena of serious interviews, indications of facial expressions, laughing, and so on detract from the substance of the interview. Here, the interviewer undermines his credibility by trying to be cute, and it doesn't serve him well. Asking about networking and fraternizing can yield wonderful stories and reveal truths about the nature of the creative life, as well as provide practical information, as it does in this case.

**I understand that the *Star Trek* series has always been willing to look at unsolicited screenplays. Why is this unusual in Hollywood?**

It's unusual because nobody else does it! *Star Trek* is famous for that. Although they do look at unsolicited screenplays, one of the problems is that a lot of writers get into a misperception that, because *Star Trek* will read scripts from unknown writers, they should write *Star Trek* episodes for whichever series it is, and that will help them break into the industry. This is a bad idea. Don't follow this route, unless you really dig *Star Trek* and you really want to write for it, because *Star Trek* scripts are not good calling card scripts in the industry if you want to be writing for an *Ally McBeal*. Even in a similar genre series, say for *X-Files,* a *Star Trek* script would not be a calling card because *Star Trek* is a very concise and limited world. Also, most of the industry won't take a *Star Trek* script very seriously, just because of its reputation for accepting scripts from the masses. So if you are interested in breaking into television, don't write for *Star Trek* if you want a broad career. Write for the hit series that are on right now, and go the original route of writing the show producers, writing agents, kicking doors until somebody opens one. A *Star Trek* script will not, generally speaking, be taken seriously by other network shows, or open any doors for you.

Also, there are certain rules at some television shows. The first assumption is the staff on the show knows the show really well, and an outsider will not be able to write the show better than the staff. The second assumption is if the producers read a script for their show and it is similar to a show they already have in development, they run the risk of being accused of plagiarism and being sued. So many of the shows' producers won't read a script for their show by anyone, but will read scripts for other popular shows. So if you write a script for *Ally McBeal,* if the *Ally McBeal* people won't read it, everyone else probably will. And if they really like your *Ally McBeal* episode, they will pay attention to you.

However, getting your script in those doors to those people is the hard part, because they all say they won't take unsolicited scripts, and they all mean it. But there are exceptions. If you contact people and you tell them how much you enjoy their work, and you sound very legitimate (as if you actually know what their work is!), there are times people will read something—not as a submission to the show, but they will just read your writing—because you impress them. If you develop those kinds of contacts, those are the contacts you can use to impress an agent. Then if an agent picks you up, the agent will submit your sample TV specs to all the network shows, and then you are in. You are no longer sending unsolicited material; you are submitting through an agent. So the trick is to make those initial contacts with show runners and people who work on these shows, and get good feedback from them. That will impress an agent enough to pick you up and run with you.

I know all this television stuff, by the way, because a friend of mine, Jeff Lowell, was breaking into television at the same time I was breaking into features. I haven't done a lot of television stuff personally, but I'm familiar with it because I've been friends with Jeff during his sort of toil up the ladder. Jeff worked on shows like "The Drew Carey Show" and "Spin City," and is a very successful television writer now.

This question is practical and opens up a whole vein of conversation with the interview subject. This screenwriter obviously has volumes of information about her business and can help new screenwriters navigate the terrain of building a career in this field.

**What is a piece of advice someone shared with you that you live by now and tell to others?**

John Daugherty was a teacher of mine at Orange Coast College, and he sat me down one day (this was like English 102) and he told me I was writing outside my vocabulary. I was hugely offended. I thought he meant I was using a thesaurus or something. I was just plain mad. But that's not what he was saying. When I started writing, I had an idea in my head of how writers were supposed to write. I was a huge Faulkner fan, and I really thought that's how writers wrote, so that's how I was striving to write. The trick is, I'm never going to be a better Faulkner than Faulkner. There already is a Faulkner, and I can't be better than he is at what he does. But I can be the best Max Adams who ever put word to page. And that's all about personal voice. John Daugherty wasn't suggesting I used a thesaurus; he was telling me I wasn't writing in my own voice. He knew my voice because I wrote numerous editorials on topics that were chosen for class, and he was telling me to use it. That is the best advice I ever got, because when I stopped trying to write the way I thought writers were supposed to sound and just started writing, I found my voice. And a writer's voice is what makes that writer unique and special. It is what people in Hollywood are searching for every day—individual voices.

This question provides a wonderful exit to what is, for the most part, an informative interview. The interview succeeds in revealing the interview subject and the intricacies of her craft and her character. The interview falls short at times by asking questions that are off the mark or vague, or including silly notes about laughing.

Let's take a minute to think about how the interview could be improved by applying the techniques in this book. First, let's look at what the interviewer did right. His paraphrased quote from William Goldman was interesting; had that question been more specifically directed, it would've drawn out a more interesting response. The best questions are the ones in which he asks about specific aspects of craft or the practical concerns of living the life of a screenwriter.

How could the tools in chapter 2 have helped this interviewer? The questions in the generative exercise provide all of the answers.

1. **What identity issues inform the writer's work (ethnicity, religious beliefs, sexuality, etc.)?**
The interviewer attempts to get at this through asking what the interviewee was like as a child. A little research might have enabled the interviewer to explore specific and relevant issues that inform the writer's work and offer the reader a more thorough and in-depth understanding of the writer.

2. **What interests inform the writer's work (travel, sports, history, etc.)?**
The writer's interest in this case is screenwriting.

3. **List five aspects of the craft of writing that you would like to discuss with this writer.**
Here's where the interviewer could've improved his work. By honing in on specific issues related to the craft of screenwriting and the craft of presenting volumes of information in her book, the interviewer could've imparted even more information in his interview.

4. **List five aspects of the creative process that you would like to discuss with this writer.**
This line of inquiry would yield useful information about the process of getting a screenplay down on paper and seeing it through from an initial idea to a final product. It is directed at providing information to the target audience of aspiring screenwriters.

5. **List five quotes from this writer's work that illustrate any of these aspects of writing.**
If the interviewer had used quotes from the book as a means of exploring issues of craft, it would accomplish two things. First, it would give readers a taste of the style of the book. Second, it would provide a way for

the interviewer to get some of the information that's in the book into his interview.

**6. List two quotes from other writers about writing in general that you would like to bring up with this writer.**

The Goldman quote is the only example of this, but having quotes from other screenwriters would raise the level of conversation, place the conversation into the larger literary dialogue, and give the interview subject something interesting to pursue.

**7. List one quote from a reviewer regarding this writer that you would like to explore with this writer in person.**

Reviewer quotes often help an interviewer articulate ideas and themes that he wants to talk about with the interview subject. Including quotes from a reviewer also lets the interview subject and the reader know that the interviewer has done his homework and read up on his subject.

**8. Are there any difficult questions (about failures, shortcomings, criticisms) you have in mind that may require diplomacy? If so, list them here.**

This would be a wonderful kind of question to interest aspiring screenwriters. Anyone who's established themselves in screenwriting must have endured all kinds of failures and challenges, as it's a notoriously difficult field. Sharing failures and strategies for overcoming challenges is one of the most interesting and inspiring things an interview can do.

**9. Are there any personal questions that you can frame in literary terms? If so, list them here.**

If any of Adams's screenplays reflected personal experiences, it would be interesting to ask her about the role of autobiography in her screenwriting. The interviewer tried to broach this subject by asking about the writer as a child, but because he hadn't done enough research to understand influences from her life on her work, he couldn't encourage an interesting response.

**10. Is there anything painfully obvious that you would like to ask (in a creative way, of course)? If so, list it here.**

Sometimes if the interviewer asks himself this question, he can come up with a couple of questions he may not have considered asking. Every tool for brainstorming questions is helpful.

# CHAPTER 9

# The Author Interview in Other Media

While the tools in this book lean toward the creation of in-depth author interviews, the same techniques can also be used to improve interviews with creative persons in theater, visual arts, dance, film, and music, for television and radio as well as print. Interviewers who work in these other media and want to improve their interviewing skills and develop a signature style of their own will benefit from the nuts-and-bolts strategies for preparing, conducting, and presenting an interview that are outlined in this book.

In addition, every interviewer can learn from watching interviews in other media, including television and radio. *Inside the Actor's Studio* is only one of many examples, including

- *Charlie Rose*
- *Larry King Live*
- *Fresh Air*
- *The Connection*

## Television Broadcasting

Authors have often been interviewed on television talk shows, including the well-known *Charlie Rose* show and C-SPAN2's *Book TV*. But the success of *Oprah's Book Club* has led to whole new wave of on-air book clubs featuring interviews with the author of a selected book. Here is a sampling of television show book clubs:

- *Today Show*
- *Good Morning America*
- *Reading with Ripa*
- *Oprah's Book Club*
- *Martha Stewart*
- *Masterpiece Theatre*
- *Jorge Ramos's Book Club*

These book clubs include a conversation with the author and often a handful of readers who come together to discuss the book.

In addition, there are many shows on air that interview other types of creative people, *Inside the Actor's Studio* being one of the most highly visible examples. Several things vary among these shows and as a result determine the type of interview that will take place:

- television show *format:* live vs. taped interviews
- *target audience*
- media sector, such as *commercial television, public television,* or *cable television*

### Format

Just like any publication, a television show has a specified format. It may be an hourlong show devoted to the book discussion group, or a fifteen-minute interview with an author, or a longer, more in-depth interview, but in any case, the format will determine the level of depth and content that can be covered. In a shorter interview, you need to focus on the most important points that you want to get across to your audience. What are the three most important things that you want to ask this author?

Format may also require breaks for commercials or station identification, and these breaks must happen gracefully within the context of the conversation. As the interviewer, it's your job to lead the author into each break and re-orient them in the conversation upon returning from a break.

Whether an interview is taped or live can determine the nature of the content you pursue and your role in keeping the conversation on track. A taped piece will be edited, so there's more room for mistakes; the interview will also be cut down to fit the specified format. A live interview, however, leaves no room for error or for going over the time limit.

### Target Audience

The target audience is the audience you hope to reach with your interview. It determines the tone, direction, and depth of a televised author interview in much the same way that the target reader determines the nature of a printed interview. For example, an author interview on *Good Morning America* will get the author to talk about what's most interesting about a book, whereas an interview with Charlie Rose or on *Book TV* will be more likely to talk in-depth with an author about issues of craft and the creative process as well as about the serious content of their work.

The target audience of *Masterpiece Theater* differs from the target audience on the *Today Show*. The *Today Show* is a morning television show geared toward mainstream viewers in the midst of getting ready for their busy days. These viewers are not looking for depth of content and coverage; they want a glimpse. They want to know what's immediately interesting about a particular author and her latest book so they can decide whether to read it or not, and so they can be aware of current events. In this case, as in the short-format interview, ask yourself what the three most important things that viewers should know about this writer or book are.

The viewers of *Masterpiece Theater,* on the other hand, are watchers of public television, and as such they're after a more in-depth kind of coverage that goes beyond superficial areas of interest to take them somewhere they couldn't go on their own. They want an author interview that is revealing in nature and that offers insights into an author's work and the means by which the author came to write a specific book. For an interview like this, you can lead the author into a much deeper conversation about her creative process and how her stories are rendered on the page.

### Commercial, Public, and Cable Television

Last, there are differences in programs that are defined by the type of television station they appear on. Commercial programming seeks to reach a much broader audience and so is less likely to delve into issues of craft or topics of particular interest to writers and intellectuals. Commercial television programs want to address the concerns of the widest possible range of viewers, and many times this means a more generalized look at an author and her work. If you are conducting an interview for commercial television, you will most likely have time constraints and specific lines of questioning that the producers want you to pursue in order to please the largest audience.

Public television, on the other hand, has room to go deeper because it aims for viewers who want their television experience to teach them something or offer something beyond what commercial television does. These viewers are interested in exploring deeper questions with a writer and hearing about the creative process and the magic that sparked a book, as much as they are interested in the more generally appealing issues.

Cable television is the land of no boundaries, and these programs are free to define their own scope and reach. Viewers of *Book TV,* for example, have to specifically subscribe for that program, so they're very likely to want to hear in-depth information on the books presented.

In conclusion, as you prepare for an interview on television or radio, you must consider the program's format, target audience, and media sector so that you can be sure to prepare questions and generate conversation appropriate to your target audience.

### Television Is Visual—How Will You Look?

You also need to consider the visual component of a televised interview. What will you wear to fit in with the look of the program? Will you hold note cards or read from a teleprompter? What do you notice about body

**Exercise for Watching a TV Interview**

- First, ask yourself the basic questions we covered earlier: What is the interview format? What is the target audience? What is the media sector?
- Did the interviewer do his homework?
- What do you notice about the interviewer's body language?
- Do you have questions after the interview that you would've liked answered?
- What can you learn from watching the interviewer at work?
- What could you do to improve this interview?

language? Here are some tips that will help you come across well on television:

- Don't fidget or tap your foot, because that makes you appear nervous.
- Sit on the edge of your chair so that you are upright and appear energized. If you sit back or slump, you come across as low energy.
- Sound upbeat and positive, but don't talk too fast, even if you have a short time slot.

*Improving Your Interview Skills by Watching TV Interviews*

Interviewers can learn a lot about the role of the interviewer and the roles of a target audience and specified format by watching TV interviews. As you watch author interviews on different programs and channels, bear in mind the format, target audience, and type of TV programming and try to understand how these factors inform the nature of the interview.

Watching televised interviews can give you ideas about how to handle interview questions that have gone awry or subjects who behave unconventionally. For example, when Robin Williams was on *Inside the Actor's Studio*, he hardly let James Lipton ask a question because he was so busy with his stream-of-consciousness comedy. Lipton encouraged Williams's spontaneity, but when he had a question that he really wanted answered, he interrupted until Williams settled down. If your author or other interview subject gets sidetracked, you can lead them back to the topics you want them to discuss by interjecting any of the following:

- "You mentioned earlier . . . could you say more about that?"
- "I want you to go back to what you were saying about . . ."
- "I loved what you said about . . ."
- "I'm interested to hear more about . . ."

A compliment can get the interview subject's attention and help them get back on track with your line of questioning.

## Radio Broadcasting

*Fresh Air* with Terry Gross is a wonderful example of what can be accomplished in a radio interview. Two things vary among these shows and as a result determine the type of interview that will take place:

- radio show *format*
- *target audience*

These factors inform the nature of the radio interview just like they do the television interview. Let's take the example of an interview that Terry Gross conducted with author Jeffrey Euginides on September 24, 2002.*

**Terry Gross, host:** This is FRESH AIR. I'm Terry Gross. You may know my guest, Jeffrey Eugenides, as the author of the novel *The Virgin Suicides,* which was adapted into a film. His second novel has just been published. It's called *Middlesex.* The narrator of the story was born in 1960, and starts life as a girl named Callie, but as she approached puberty, she realizes that she isn't like other girls. Eventually she discovers that she was born a hermaphrodite, and she is becoming more physically masculine with age. In her early teens, she abandons her identity as a woman and changes her name from Callie to Cal and begins to live as a man. The novel also covers the two preceding generations of the narrator's family, starting with his Greek immigrant parents. *New York Times* book critic Michiko Kakutani writes, "The novel turns the story of Cal's coming of age into an uproarious epic, at once funny and sad, about misplaced identities and family secrets. Eugenides has delivered a deeply affecting portrait of one family's tumultuous engagement with the American 20th century." Let's start with a reading from *Middlesex.*

This biographical introduction uses the narrative format to mention his previous novel and to describe *Middlesex* in such a way as to provide background for listeners who haven't read the book. A quote from a reviewer offers a wonderful description of the celebrated book. The narrative introduction is a brief 175 words. Because this is a radio show, the interviewer has to fit all of the critical information into a short period of time. Starting with a reading from the novel further locates the listener in the context of the upcoming conversation. The reading gives a feel for both the story and the writer.

**Mr. Jeffrey Eugenides (Author, *Middlesex*):** "I was born twice, first as a baby girl on the remarkably smogless Detroit day in January of 1960, and then again as a teen-age boy in an emergency room near Petoskey, Michigan,

---

*Interview © 2002 by WHYY. *Fresh Air* with Terry Gross produced in Philadelphia by WHYY.

in August of 1974. Specialized readers may have come across me in Dr. Peter Luce's study 'Gender Identity in 5-Alpha-Reductase Pseudohermaphrodites,' published in the *Journal of Pediatric Endocrinology* in 1975. Or maybe you've seen my photograph in chapter 16 of the now sadly outdated *Genetics and Heredity.* That's me on page 578 standing naked beside a height chart, with a black box covering my eyes.

   "My birth certificate lists my name as Calliope Helen Stephanides. My most recent driver's license from the Federal Republic of Germany records my first name simply as Cal. I'm a former field hockey goalie, long-standing member of the Save-the-Manatee Foundation, rare attendant at the Greek Orthodox liturgy and, for most of my adult life, an employee of the U.S. State Department. Like Tiresias, I was first one thing and then the other. I've been ridiculed by classmates, guinea pigged by doctors, palpated by specialists, and researched by the March of Dimes. A red-headed girl from Grosse Point fell in love with me, not knowing what I was; her brother liked me, too. An Army tank led me into urban battle once. A swimming pool turned me into myth. I've left my body in order to occupy others, and all this happened before I turned 16."

   **Gross:** That's Jeffrey Eugenides reading the beginning of his new novel *Middlesex.* Jeffrey, why did you want to write about a contemporary hermaphrodite?

Here Gross restates the context for listeners who've just tuned in who may be wondering what's going on. She opens with a general but very relevant question about the unusual subject of the book. What people may really want to know is whether or not *he* is a hermaphrodite, but that would be too personal and inappropriate. This question opens the door for the writer to talk about his interest in his subject.

   **Mr. Eugenides:** Well, the first kernel of the idea came to me when I read an actual memoir of a 19th-century hermaphrodite that Michelle Foucault found in the archives of the French Public Department of Hygiene. And I thought this would be a very interesting book, and went and read it and was filled with frustration, because the hermaphrodite in question, Herculine Barbin, was a convent schoolgirl, or at least in her early years, and when she came to write the story of her life, she wrote very much like a convent schoolgirl. I actually brought the diary with me in case you wanted to hear some of it. But she . . .

His response answers that personal question right away and also shows a lot about the writer's process for research and generating ideas.

   **Gross:** Oh, you bet.
   **Mr. Eugenides:** Oh, OK.

**Gross:** Why don't you read a few lines from it?

**Mr. Eugenides:** I will. This is midway through her memoirs when she has fallen in love with her best friend at the convent school, and this is the first night they spend together.

"Happy about this pretext, which was only too true, one evening I asked my friend to share my bed. She accepted with pleasure. It would be impossible to express the happiness I felt from her presence at my side. I was wild with joy. We talked for a long time before going to sleep, I with my arms encircling her waist, she with her face resting near my own. My God, was I guilty? And must I accuse myself here of a crime? No, no, that fault was not mine. It was the fault of an unexampled fatality which I could not resist!!! Henceforth, Sarah belonged to me!! She was mine!!!"

It sort of goes on in that fashion, and I was just terribly frustrated because she was evasive about her story, and all of the things I wanted to know about a hermaphrodite's life she was unable to tell me. And I got the idea of writing my own story, and in contrast with the way most hermaphrodites in literature have been handled, usually as mythical creatures or as fanciful creations like Orlando in Virginia Woolf, I wanted to write a story about a real-life hermaphrodite and be as accurate as I could about the medical facts and the biological circumstances.

Here Eugenides offers a glimpse of the work that inspired his novel and goes on to explain how the missing pieces in the girl's narrative made him want to write a story that created a real hermaphroditic character. The drive to create what's missing, and what one most wants to know, is a common phenomenon among writers. Sena Jeter Naslund, in her interview in *Conversations with American Women Writers,* describes how the impulse to write *Ahab's Wife* developed from her dissatisfaction with the fact that there was no strong female character in *Moby Dick* with whom her young daughter could identify. She wanted to create the missing woman who was Ahab's wife, who was only mentioned in a sentence.

**Gross:** What's the medical explanation for your main character's condition?

Now the interviewer moves into a question about the details of the subject matter, figuring, perhaps, that most listeners will not know that much about what makes a hermaphrodite the way s/he is.

**Mr. Eugenides:** Well, it's a very rare genetic mutation, and the condition is called 5-alpha-reductase deficiency syndrome. And it occurs in very isolated communities. What it basically is, if you inherit this mutation, your body is unable to respond to certain androgens, or male hormones, for a long time, and as you're formed in the womb, if you would have an XY chromosome, you would be male, and you would be born looking very, very much like a girl, almost undetectably so. And at puberty, as testosterone gets stronger in your blood, you would then virilize and become quite masculine in appearance. So it's one of the most dramatic hermaphroditic conditions that exists, and that's one of the reasons it appealed to me. But in that it was usually occurring only in in-bred communities and isolated communities, I then saw a chance to broaden this story from a fictional memoir of a hermaphrodite to a story about an entire family, a Greek American family in this case, and the transmission of this gene down through the generations until it finally is inherited by the narrator and flowers in her body, and later as a man, she tells the story.

The writer answers the medical question and brings it back to how the medical information helped him to shape and develop his narrative. This is interesting, because many readers believe that ideas come out of thin air, when in fact the writer's imagination is often grounded in real events.

**Gross:** And since this genetic condition happens in in-bred populations, you have this character's grandparents being not only husband and wife, but also brother and sister, and the characters' parents are not only husband and wife, but also second cousins. Why did you want to explore that kind of familial marital relationship?

Gross is trying to get at the impulse for the writer to explore such an unusual family structure. She gives background so that the listeners who haven't read the book will understand where the question comes from.

**Mr. Eugenides:** Well, the inbreeding was demanded by the genetic condition I was using, and to bring in mythology again, of course, Zeus and Hera, I believe, are brother and sister in Greek mythology, and so I was playing with some of these ancient ideas in literature. I needed to dramatize inbreeding, and inbreeding is actually quite boring. It takes generations and generations and centuries, and so in order to dramatize that, it required me to speed up the process and to actually have grandparents be siblings. It seemed to me to be the best way to dramatize, you know, what was going on at a cellular level.

Eugenides is a wonderful interviewee in that he truly stays focused on talking about the work of writing and how he came to the particulars of his novel. Rather than offering a quick answer about how inbreeding was demanded by the genetic condition, he discusses the role of mythology and how he was playing with ancient archetypes as well. He goes on to further elucidate how the facts of his subject determined the imaginative context of the novel.

**Gross:** Jeffrey Eugenides is my guest. He's the author of the book *The Virgin Suicides*. Now he has a new novel called *Middlesex* about a hermaphrodite.

Now in the beginning of your book *Middlesex*, the narrator explains that he was born as a girl and reborn as a teen-age boy in an emergency room at the age of 14. What happens in the emergency room?

Again, because this is radio, Terry Gross reminds her listeners who she's talking to before launching into another question, which begins with a brief paraphrasing from the opening of the book. She then wants to know what happens in the emergency room in order to explore the transition of the character's gender identity.

**Mr. Eugenides:**  Well, in the emergency room is the first time when someone other than Callie sees her anatomy in bright light. At that point, Callie is 14, she still looks like a girl, though a flat-chested one, but after an accident, she's taken to the emergency room and in undressing her to see if she has any broken bones, the doctor does see her genitals which, at that point, would be not characteristic, or entirely characteristic, of a girl of her age.
**Gross:**  And why does your character decide to be a boy?

These questions are drawing Eugenides into talking about the story rather than about creating the story. One wonders how Terry Gross sees her role as author interviewer. Is it to get the author talking about the story in order to expose listeners to interesting literature? Is it to learn something more about the story than they would know after reading it themselves? Is it to understand the writer's muse and the creative spirit? Or is she exploring the reality of the life of the hermaphrodite? Perhaps all of the above.

**Mr. Eugenides:**  Well, it's a long process and a difficult one for her. The condition that she has, of course, is so virilizing that after she goes through puberty, she would basically have musculature, facial hair, and a deep voice and would appear to be male. So it would be easier at least to operate in society as a male. And Cal, as he talks about his life in Berlin as an adult, he's careful to say that he operates in society as a male. It's not clear whether he considers himself a regular man or a regular guy, but it is the way that he most easily can get along.

The author's answer doesn't tell us anything we couldn't know from reading the book. If Gross is out to expose listeners to interesting literature straight from the writer's mouth, she's succeeding. Otherwise, she's not gaining any deeper insight into the novel than a reader could get on his own.

**Gross:** He seems to have a consciousness of what he is, which is something that's strictly neither a hundred percent male nor a hundred percent female.

Here she's trying to go deeper by diving into the character's psyche to understand how he perceives his gender identity.

**Mr. Eugenides:** Right. But I think in terms of the book itself, because Callie falls in love with her best friend, that that did provide a certain impetus for her decision to be a boy. But then, of course, when she goes to the sexual agenda identity clinic, she does find out about her chromosomal status being XY, and that is another reason why she finally decides to adopt a male gender identity.

Again, there's nothing new in his response beyond what any reader could gather for herself.

**Gross:** When she decides to adopt a male gender identity, she has to learn the outward characteristics of men. I want you read a paragraph—this is on page 449—in which your main character describes that kind of transformation of learning to walk and talk like a male.

Now, as the person analyzing this interview, I think that she's most interested in letting her listeners in on what's so interesting about this story in the hopes of exposing them to compelling literature.

**Mr. Eugenides:** "Like a convert to a new religion, I overdid it at first. Somewhere near Gary, Indiana, I adopted a swagger. I rarely smiled. My expression throughout Illinois was the Clint Eastwood squint. It was all bluff, but so was it on most men. We were all walking around squinting at each other. My swagger wasn't that different from what lots of adolescent boys put on trying to be manly. For that reason, it was convincing. Its very falseness made it credible. Now and then I fell out of character. Feeling something stuck to the bottom of my shoe, I kicked up my heel and looked back over my shoulder to see what it was, rather than crossing my leg in front of me and twisting up my shoe. I picked correct change from my open palm instead of my trouser pocket.

Such slips made me panic, but needlessly. No one noticed. I was aided by that. As a rule, people don't notice much."

This is a wonderful passage that is well-placed to illustrate what the interviewer means. Having the author read passages on air works in much the same way that quotes work in printed interviews.

**Gross:** I'm wondering if when you wrote that, you thought back to your own puberty and when you were going through the process of turning into a man from having been a boy, and if you felt that you were acting in a way, acting the role of man.

Now she succeeds in really plumbing the depths of both the creation of that moment in the text and the author's own relationship to that material.

**Mr. Eugenides:** This continues to be something that I feel like I do. In order to get those characteristics that I thought were more common amongst females than males, I didn't think back to my early years. I actually walked around my room trying to imagine how do girls usually look at things when they're stuck to their shoe? How do they count change? And it actually took me a long time to come up with just those few examples that seemed to me evidently female or male.

This response reveals exactly how the author came up with those telling physical details that describe character. Through physically acting things out, the author was able to connect with the action in some deeper way that enabled him to write the character.

**Gross:** For your novel *Middlesex,* you've really mastered a lot of the medical language of the contemporary hermaphrodite. You know a lot about the intersex support groups. What kind of research did you do so that you would have both a medical and social understanding of what hermaphrodites might be going through today?

This is a question of process that addresses the particulars of his subject, seeking to uncover how Eugenides acquired enough knowledge to create the character of Callie.

**Mr. Eugenides:** Well, the debate right now in terms of intersex people, and in terms of sexual reconfiguration surgery, is between the pediatric endocrinologists and the hermaphrodites, or the intersex community. So I basically read text from both sides of that debate. I read a lot of sexology. I read books by John Money, who's the leading theoretician in the sexology field, or has been. And I read a lot of things published by the Intersex Society of North America based out in San Francisco, and corresponded briefly with the executive director of that organization. And they have a newsletter that is called "Hermaphrodites With Attitude," and they also publish other books and writings by hermaphrodites. So I read all of those. I watched videos that they offer about hermaphrodites telling their own stories. And I left it at that. I didn't interview intersex people, and I didn't go on the road to visit their demonstrations. I tried to acquire the knowledge through reading what they had to say and then imagining the rest myself.

Interestingly, the author chose not to meet intersex people but rather to study and read and fill his mind with their reality, leaving the actual physical incarnation to his imagination and the page. This question worked well in getting at his choices and attitudes as regards research.

**Gross:** Why didn't you want to go to the demonstrations or meet any intersex people?

Gross seems to want more information. A better approach might be to acknowledge the response and then ask him to say more about it. For example, "Can you say more about how meeting intersex people interferes with your creative process? Why is it essential to rely on your imagination?"

**Mr. Eugenides:** I just don't usually work in the entirely reportorial mode. I need a certain amount of information, but I work largely through my imagination and through a sort of method acting where I try to imagine if I put myself into this situation, how would I have reacted? And in that way, I hope that the story seems more believable. And I don't try to look at another person and try to imagine what it's like for them. If I had been a hermaphrodite, this is what I would have been like, and it may not be the way other intersex people are, but it certainly is the way that this character would have been. Because I also don't believe that there is any one experience that would be the intersex or hermaphrodite experience. There would be just as many as any other population, just as various.

**Gross:** At the same time you were reading the sexology literature and the intersex literature, were you also reading ancient Greek literature?

Both this question and the following answer are helpful in that they explore the Greek literary and mythological axis of the novel as well as the author's early interest in this subject matter.

**Mr. Eugenides:** I didn't read a lot of ancient Greek literature while writing *Middlesex*, but I took seven years of Latin. I started studying Latin in seventh grade, and this influenced my writing quite a bit. In fact, I was just thinking the other day, in tenth grade, our Latin teacher had us read Ovid's *Metamorphosis*, and we were reading about the argument between Zeus and Hera and the argument was about who had the most pleasure in the act of love, men or women. Zeus said men did; Hera said women did. And they argue and then they decide, "Well, let's ask Tiresias." Tiresias was both man and woman. Tiresias is brought in and says, "Women enjoy the great part of pleasure in lovemaking."

As you can imagine, this was of great interest to the young Latin scholar that I was in tenth grade, and probably, in a way, started me thinking about Tiresias, hermaphrodites, and the whole issue of what it would be like if you were a person who could experience both realms.

**Gross:** While we're talking about gender, which is the subject that you write about both in *The Virgin Suicides* and in your new novel *Middlesex*, I'm wondering if when you were growing up, there were aspects of masculinity you felt you didn't fit into, and if there were things about being female that particularly interested you, that you particularly would have liked to either experience or understand more?

This question seeks to understand the author as the source of the quandaries in his work. She asks a very personal question about the author's early gender experiences. I would not recommend that anyone other than Terry Gross do this. At its most basic, this question asks what in the author's life made him explore these ideas about gender in his novels. If you were in the position of asking this personal question, how could you use the tools we've discussed to get away with it? One way would be to raise the conversation into the larger context of literature by using quotes from other writers or quotes from books on writing.

**Mr. Eugenides:** I mean, actually I've always been quite happy in my gender. I was very interested in sports as a boy, and the only thing that I did that was not terribly masculine was that I had a great interest in theater. And when you are acting and in theater, you are, in some ways, going away from the normal route of young boys. But I don't remember wanting to do things that girls did, or anything like that. In fact, when I was about 12 or 13, I had very long hair, and was sometimes mistaken for a girl. If I were with a group of girls, a mother would come out and she would say, "Would you girls like some Kool-Aid?" and I would absolutely be horrified by this. So I was pretty Midwestern in wanting to be a boy and pretty happy with that.

**Gross:** You're been living in Berlin for at least a couple of years. How long has it been?

Gross now pursues an interesting fact about the author that is not related to his work. Again, the type of interview that Gross conducts is aimed at educating her audience about the author and his latest work rather than the inner workings of craft and creativity, though she touches on those subjects too.

**Mr. Eugenides:** We're starting our fourth year. We've been here three years, which is much longer than we ever thought. We were originally coming just for one year on a grant, but we've liked the city and so we've stayed on.

**Gross:** And, you know, at this time, when you've been writing about the history of immigrants in America and what gender is like in America, you've actually been living far from America in Berlin. And I'm wondering if you feel like you've been living in an environment in which gender expectations are slightly different than in the United States.

Gross again pursuing interesting information related by theme to his book but really not about his book or his writing. It is more about his life and his perceptions of the world he currently inhabits. She's following her nose here, probing around in an effort to draw a connection between his experience and his writing.

**Mr. Eugenides:** Well, one thing I first have to say about the experience of living in Berlin, there's a famous—not a famous story, there's a story in my family about my grandparents. When they first came to the United States, my grandfather had to do all the shopping because he could speak English and my grandmother couldn't, and she was frightened of the stores. And so he basically was the public face for the family. He would talk to anyone on the phone. He would do the shopping. He would deal with salesmen and things like that. And because I started my German a little bit before Karen, my wife, did, for the first years in Berlin, I was also this immigrant who could half speak the language and had to do all of those things.

So when I was writing about my grandparents in Detroit getting used to Detroit, I was actually in a similar experience as an immigrant or as a foreigner in Germany.

His answer yields information that is relevant to his book, and her probing has paid off with this final reward.

**Exercise**

Analyze the Eugenides interview, making your own observations about the interviewer's style.
- Who is her target audience? Does she succeed in addressing them?
- What does she do as a requirement of her radio format?
- What can you learn from the interviewer, Terry Gross? What does she do well? What does she do that you can incorporate into your own work?
- What do you think she could do better? Do you have questions that weren't answered? Were there areas you would like her to have explored? What techniques have you learned that would improve her interview?
- Do you consider this a successful interview?

**Gross:** I would imagine one of the most frustrating things about that is that when you can't speak the language of a country, a lot of people just assume that you're not very smart.

**Mr. Eugenides:** That you're dumb.

**Gross:** Yeah, because you can't articulate what you're thinking . . .

**Mr. Eugenides:** Yes.

**Gross:** . . . or even what you want to buy in the grocery store.

**Mr. Eugenides:** Yes. And a fact about Berlin that might not be known is that Berliners are the rudest people on the planet. They make New Yorkers seem like they have Southern charm. And if you don't speak properly, and if you dawdle, you will receive a tongue-lashing that you can't imagine.

**Gross:** Or that you can't understand, either, if you don't speak the language.

**Mr. Eugenides:** Well, you can get the gist of it, believe me.

**Gross:** Right. Well, Jeffrey Eugenides, thank you very much for talking with us.

**Mr. Eugenides:** Thank you. I really enjoyed it.

**Gross:** Jeffrey Eugenides is the author of the new novel *Middlesex*. I'm Terry Gross, and this is FRESH AIR.

This whole last exchange is conversation directed at winding down the interview. In a printed interview, the interviewer would edit these unrelated remarks out of the final piece.

# CHAPTER 10

# The Art of the Author Interview in the Writing Program

## M.F.A. Program

Learning interdisciplinary skills that will fuel one's creative work is critical for any writer interested in sustaining a literary life. These skills include interviewing, writing reviews, editing or working at a literary publication, teaching, and studying the other arts.

Teaching student writers the art of the author interview can arm them with the tools they need to continue their creative lives and create support once they move beyond the graduate writing program into the wider world. Many students attend M.F.A. programs for both the education and the literary community, as most otherwise write in isolation in the midst of lives populated with folks who don't understand the particularities of the writer's struggle.

As I mentioned earlier, the author interview provides an opportunity for the new writer to build a literary life that can sustain her work for the long haul once her writing program is over. By engaging in critical study, talking with an admired writer, publishing and working with editors, and gaining visibility in the literary world, a new author creates for herself the critical aspects of the M.F.A. program that supported her for two years.

In addition, interviewing authors gets students enthused and inspired about their own work. The feeling of proximity to a successful writer helps them understand that they, too, can get there if they're willing to work toward their goals.

This section will cover the many ways of incorporating *The Art of the Author Interview* into an M.F.A. program.

### Program Models

There are many ways that M.F.A. programs can weave author interviewing into their curricula. For instance, faculty can invite a professional writer who regularly conducts author interviews and might offer expertise and insight to students; she can teach a seminar or workshop, or work with students over the course of an interview project. Some programs will offer the author interview as a regular component, and others will offer it intermittently, depending on demand.

Lesley University's low-residency M.F.A. program, for example, offers The Art of the Author Interview regularly, as students are required to complete three credits of interdisciplinary study. As an interdisciplinary faculty member, I conduct an Art of the Author Interview workshop during a biannual residency with the students whom I will be working with remotely during the course of the semester. Then we touch base once a month to answer questions and keep their projects on track. At the end of the semester they've conducted and created a publishable author interview with an author they admire. Students can interview faculty members or any established author that agrees to an interview. Also, since I advise new author interviewers to use their own connections to reach authors, the program director has started building a database of writers who are reachable through faculty members, visiting faculty, and others associated with the program, helping students to get important access to authors.

The M.F.A. program at Antioch in Los Angeles intermittently offers an author interview workshop, as well as other interdisciplinary workshops in the arts of writing book reviews, editing literary journals, and pursuing other professions suited to writers with M.F.A.'s. This program feature is called "Writers at Work."

Other writing programs have regular faculty who are experienced in interviewing authors and who offer their expertise via lectures, seminars, or workshops. Oftentimes a student may opt to conduct an interview in place of the semester's critical paper, as the interview requires the same type of critical reading and analytical thinking.

Whether the art of interviewing authors is offered regularly or now and again, it can make a huge difference in how the writing student views her life beyond the writing program. By learning to incorporate the professional arts into the creative arts, new writers can build a literary life that will help them meet their professional and creative goals, and if teaching students how to continue learning and living the life of the writer is one of the goals of the M.F.A. program, then the possibility of interviewing authors should at least be introduced.

*Program Ideas*

There are as many ways to incorporate author interviews into an M.F.A. program as there are M.F.A. programs and students, so your program should be able to introduce the idea of interviewing authors in a way that meets your budgetary and curricula restraints.

WORKSHOPS, LECTURES, SEMINARS. These offer students the nuts-and-bolts information they need in order to make contact with an author, prepare for, and conduct a successful interview. Almost every writer I know has, at some point, wanted to interview another author but has never gone through with it, fearing that there was something to it that they didn't know how to do. Arming students with the information they need to succeed empowers them to go after the interview and produce successful results. I'm constantly surprised by the level of work my students produce once their questions have been answered and their fears alleviated.

The workshops, lectures, or seminars can be offered by regular faculty or visiting experts and should be aimed at preparing students to take on an actual project with the support of the expert or their faculty advisor.

STUDYING AUTHOR INTERVIEWS IN PRINT. There are many wonderful collections of author interviews and interviews with other creative people that can be instructive to writing students and especially those who hope to conduct interviews. Literary journals and magazines also publish author interviews on a regular basis.

By studying these resources, students and aspiring writers and artists can
- internalize the pacing and flow of an effective interview
- understand the many kinds of questions that can be asked
- see the interviewer's research at work
- study the interplay between interviewer and interviewee, question and answer
- learn how to use quotes effectively
- get ideas for new directions in their own interviews
- develop their own ideas about what makes a great interview
- inform their own creative work
- get answers to technical questions about craft
- learn about the life of the writer and the creative process

STUDYING AUTHOR INTERVIEWS ON VIDEO. Interviews on video also provide an effective educational environment, in that the student can observe the unedited interview itself. Even though the video will most likely have been edited for time and other concerns, it will not have been edited in the same rigorous way that a print interview is (by both interviewer and author). A video interview cannot delete words or change punctuation. When a student watches a video interview, she sees how the author speaks and the interviewer's and author's body language, and she hears the verbal ticks, the ums, ahs, likes, and so on. This is invaluable for preparing the student for the difference between the spoken event and the written event. Additionally, watching the live interview on video exposes the student to how the interviewer handles digressions, when he chooses to interject or not interject, and how, in general, he handles himself during the interview. In other words, the student can see the professionalism (or lack thereof) of the interviewer.

INTERVIEWING FACULTY MEMBERS. This is a comfortable way for students to become familiar with the interview process that works well for a couple of reasons. First, students feel more comfortable with established writers in their own sphere, with whom they have perhaps studied. Also, it's easier for them to contact and set up the interview with someone they know. Since, in most cases, this will be their first interview, they don't have the credentials to secure interviews with writers outside their day-to-day lives.

The M.F.A. program at Hamline University has students interview faculty members (or anyone else with whom they can secure an interview). The students work with a faculty member over the course of the semester to develop and conduct their interview, and the final interviews are published in the program's literary journal *WaterStone*.

I'm currently working on a project at the Bennington College Writing Seminars M.F.A. Program that my friend, the poet and arts visionary Jason Shinder, developed whereby students interview faculty members under my tutelage and compile the finished procucts in an anthology celebrating the ten-year anniversary of the program.

INTERVIEWING VISITING FACULTY. This enables the student to step outside his comfort zone and interview a writer he doesn't know personally or see every day. This can be an exciting experience for the new writer, as it places him face to face with an author of some distinction. By preparing for the interview and composing the questions, the student imbibes the author's work in a way that will inform and fuel his own work. Then he has the added benefit of being able to sit down and talk with this author in an intelligent forum. The resultant interview can be developed for publication and a new relationship or link is established between the student and the writer.

Once the student has stepped beyond his comfort zone, he's ready to broaden the circle and perhaps contact an author through connections with other authors or though a publicist.

LIVE INTERVIEWS WITH FACULTY OR VISITING WRITERS. Live interviews offer an engaging way to explore the art of the author interview in an educational forum, along the lines of *Inside the Actors' Studio*. One person conducts the interview, either a visiting interviewer, faculty member, or student. The interview subject can be a faculty member, visiting faculty member, or another author contacted for the occasion of the live interview. The interview should be conducted in front of an audience of M.F.A. students who can listen to the interview and notice the work of the interviewer and how that affects the nature of the responses. Students should be instructed ahead of time to think critically of the interview from what they've learned through studying author interviews. After the interview, students are encouraged to ask questions of the interviewer as well as the interview subject. The interview can be recorded or videotaped for use later in the classroom. It can give invaluable feedback to the interviewer about her performance, questions, and manner on film.

INTERVIEWING NATIONALLY RECOGNIZED WRITERS. A program with nationally recognized authors as regular faculty offers a rare opportunity to the writing student to take on an interview with a writer they would not otherwise have access to. If the program does not have nationally recognized writers, then setting up these interviews takes more involvement on the part of the educator.

I've used my credentials or connections to secure interviews for students interviewing nationally recognized authors. If faculty members are willing to help students make connections beyond the program, this can work. Often an author will agree when the work is part of a writing program, and when the student is working with a professional. I'd only suggest making matches between authors and students who are truly up to the task of examining that author's work and carrying on the necessary conversation. Students need to have a positive, successful experience to continue this work and have it contribute to their writing lives.

INTERVIEW CHAPBOOKS. So now what do you do with all of these student author interviews? Publishing a chapbook of student interviews can be a great motivator for the students, and a final reward. A chapbook release party at the end of the semester or year appreciating the great work that students are doing can help keep everyone excited about their interdisciplinary projects and encourage them to continue this important work.

## The Undergraduate Writing Program

The undergraduate writing program can use all of the program ideas recommended for the graduate writing program. In addition, some introductory programming ideas can provide the foundation for more advanced work.

### Beginner Program Ideas

HANDS-ON WORKSHOPS. Through hands-on workshops that include reading interviews and writing responses or completing generative exercises like those in this book, students can begin to learn the art of the author interview. Workshops can include instruction on how to write an effective query letter, how to record an interview, and how to address the technical aspects of an interview, including format and length.

INTERVIEWING EACH OTHER. By interviewing each other about anything from reading preferences, to political beliefs or early life experiences, students can get a feel for how the question and answer format works. They learn firsthand how their questions affect the interview subject and the nature of responses they can expect. If students record and transcribe these interviews, then work to edit them into a final written piece, they will learn how the conversation leads to the final written version of the interview. This is useful in illustrating for the student how the final sparkling piece emerges from a possibly messy conversation.

# Final Thoughts and Interview Tips

Only you can decide the kind of interview you want to do. Only you can set the standards for your work. Of course, you have to balance your ideals against the realities of publishing and the literary world. For instance, if you don't care about publishing your interviews, you have more freedom than if you hope to publish, in which case you'll have to find publications that are a good match for your type of interview. In many cases, you'll modify your style to meet the editorial guidelines of the publications in which you hope to publish your interviews.

In thinking about the type of interview you would like to do, ask yourself the following questions:

- How much preparation are you willing to do?
- How long an interview are you interested in doing?
- Where are you interested in publishing?
- Who would you like to read your interview?
- Who would you like to interview?
- How would you like your interview process to inform your own professional life?

The answers to these questions will help you to zero in on the kind of interview you want to do and inform your editorial choices.

## Rejection As Information

Remember that if your interview is rejected, that rejection is providing you with valuable information. Rejection happens for many reasons, including the following, all of which are useful to know about if you're serious about your work:

- You submitted to a publication that is unsuitable for your interview. For example, you submitted a 7,000-word in-depth author interview to a regional newspaper that covers literary subject matter.
- Your work is not up to the standards of the publication where you submitted.

- The publication has scheduled their interviews into the next three years.
- Your interview does not meet the editorial preferences of the publication. For example, it only publishes interviews with writers who have a book coming out.

All of these circumstances tell you something about where you're submitting your work or about its quality. Addressing them in advance will hlep you get your work accepted.

## Common Problems

There are several problems common to author interviews and other interviews with creative people. Identifying these problems and understanding them now can help you avoid them in your own interviews.

### Lack of Preparation

An interviewer's lack of preparation can doom an interview. Poor preparation will be evident in flat questions that don't reveal anything new about the writer. The unprepared interviewer will rely heavily on the author's press kit and other writings about the writer, rather than reading the writer's work with a critical eye and forming his own questions. The questions will thus be brief and thin, not offering any new information and not extracting it.

Every interviewer has time constraints that limit the amount and quality of research they can do for an interview, especially if he is working on a deadline for a specific, regularly published magazine. Even someone without a lot of time can do adequate research if he knows how to focus and go about that research with a trained eye. Using the generative exercises throughout this book will help you create an effective, compelling interview even when you are operating under a tight deadline.

### Disorganization

Interviews often have an assortment of questions, some of which employ the principles of this book and work well, others that may be off track but are included in the interview nonetheless. These interviewers present these questions in a seemingly random order, without thought to the flow of conversation. The disorganization might include a lack of balance in the coverage of the author's books, undue emphasis on an early work and silence on a more recent work, or a fixation on theme over craft or process over technique. Imbalance is the sign of a disorganized mind. Once your questions are composed to your satisfaction, take the time to stand back and organize the flow of the interview. Remember, your questions are the road map to the conversation. After you've transcribed the interview, look again at the order of the material and create an effective and natural flow for the final written piece.

### Inarticulate Questions

Oftentimes questions are right on track but the interviewer hasn't taken the time to articulate them in a thoughtful manner. Readers are as interested in the questions as they are in the answers, and a well-articulated question can instill confidence in readers and let them know that they are in the hands of a real professional.

### Inappropriate Questions

Questions that are too personal, off the subject of the interview, intrusive, or out of synch with the rest of the conversation can alienate your interview subject, creating a distance that will not serve the interview well. By focusing on her work and demonstrating that you're well prepared through your thoughtful questions, you'll earn the interview subject's trust and get a much better interview in the end.

### Interview Is Too Faithful to Spoken Event

David Fenza comments: "Another common problem is that the submitted interview is too faithful to the actual spoken event. The level of diction is low; the rhetoric is clumsy, halting, verbose. Interviews can be edited for the sake of clarity and concision and still remain conversational in tone and lively."

A written interview that remains too faithful to the spoken event is really more of a transcript of a conversation. Part of your work is to edit the interview to a literary standard, re-ordering questions as needed.

### Too Much Analysis

Sometimes, a really smart well-prepared interviewer will spend too much time on a close reading of a work, which presumes that the reader will have read that work. Interviews with poets especially can often become rather microscopic in their focus. Although this may be acceptable at some journals, we [*The Writer's Chronicle*] prefer an interview that is more generally open and generally engaging— an interview that provides a introduction to the writer as an interesting thinker— an interview that might compel a reader to read the writer's work for the first time. We prefer an interview that illuminates the artist. Analysis of difficult passages, or close readings, I feel, are best left to essays.

These comments from David Fenza outline very clearly the mistake of too much analysis. Questions about writing and the writing process work well for readers who haven't read the books being discussed, and using quotes from texts can help locate the reader in the context of the conversation. Minute observation, however, can leave many readers out of the conversation. Keep your interview engaging and offer a glimpse of the artist at work without focusing on the minute details that make up that work. This is not to say that you shouldn't focus on particulars when discussing issues of craft, as this is important for both the reader and the author. But focusing on micro-details will generally not work well in the interview format.

*Self-Promotion by Interviewer*

The role of the interviewer is to stay out of the limelight while drawing the writer into conversation with the intent of presenting him and his ideas in the best light. Interviewers who only want to celebrate their proximity to a famous author or display their own intellectual prowess need to reel themselves in and rethink their role in the interview process. Perhaps Fenza puts it best:

The awful interviewer mainly wants to celebrate his or her own kinship with the famous author; or they keep showing-off their profound understanding of the author's work; these interviewers should be punished. A good interviewer should be self-effacing; the good interviewer helps the authors present their sensibilities in the best light possible. If the interviewer tries to upstage the subject, the interviewer is an ass. Interviewing is a humble occupation, like writing criticism.

*Too Much Commitment to the List of Questions*

Interviewers who hold to their list of questions as if to a lifeboat will not be open to other interesting directions their interview could explore. The interviewer needs to focus on listening to the answers of the interview subject in the hopes of taking the interview in unexpected directions. The list of questions is nothing more than a map to return to when the conversation needs to get back on track, and as such, it actually allows the interviewer the freedom to explore other avenues of conversation.

## What to Do When You're Out of Time

When you've run out of time to finish your research, whether due to poor planning or to a huge amount of information to study and understand, there are ways to focus your work to create your questions. First, think about the kinds of questions you need:
- a couple of general opening questions
- questions about craft

- questions about process and technique
- questions about each book
- questions about influences
- closing questions

Then use the generative exercises in earlier chapters to create questions that incorporate quotes from the books, from reviewers, or from other writers or artists. You can often find provocative quotes in reviews and then find questions about craft, technique, influences, and so on to ask using that quote as an illustration. Quotes from reviewers offer critical statements to which an author can respond. These responses often take the conversation in interesting directions. Of course, if you haven't done as much research as you should have, you may get lost in the new terrain, but there should be something in the author's words that you can pick up on. Quotes from other writers or artists also offer ideas to get the interview subject thinking and talking. If you're serious about conducting interviews, you can have books on craft with underlined passages that you can use in your interviews.

By gathering as much information as you can about the books and using the information and research that you *have* been able to do, you can often piece together a compelling interview. You will certainly put together an interview that will be better than most, because you've incorporated these important principles into developing the conversation.

# The History of the Author Interview

*The Paris Review* has set the standard for what a literary interview should be, and all editors can only hope to publish interviews as thought-provoking. If you read an interview in *The Paris Review,* chances are you will want to revisit that writer's work; the really great interview will help you read a writer with greater sensitivity and appreciation.

—David Fenza, editor of *The Writer's Chronicle*

## George Plimpton and the *Paris Review*

In 1953 the first issue of the *Paris Review* was released. It was a new literary quarterly with the unconventional policy of publishing creative fiction and poetry rather than the criticism typical of other literary magazines of the day. The *Paris Review* had the revolutionary idea that instead of publishing criticism, they would talk directly to the authors about their methods and intentions in their work. Using the interview form, George Plimpton and Peter Matthiessen, co-founders of the journal, hoped to elucidate the inner workings of the writer's mind so that readers could see why the words were placed on the page the way they were. Rather than seeking to criticize, the interviewers sought to understand, and through that effort they broadened the international dialogue about writing and brought crucial conversations from the private studios of the world's most famous authors out into the public domain.

The *Paris Review* interviews are the standard by which all other author interviews are measured, and they certainly deserve any serious interviewer's consideration. Over the years, the interviews have been anthologized into *Writers at Work,* a series of over ten collections of interviews. The first author the *Paris Review* interviewed was E. M. Forster, the greatest living author at the time. Forster hadn't published a novel since 1924, and this interview raised an incredible stir because in it Forster discussed the problems that made it so difficult for him to write fiction. This first interview, conducted by P. N. Furbank and F. J. H. Haskel, furnished the format for the famous interviews that would follow. These early interviews involved one interviewer asking questions and the other furiously taking notes; the author would answer in intermittent bursts, ever thoughtful of the note-taker. With the increased use of the tape recorder, interviews generally took on a more leisurely flow that resembles actual conversation. William Styron, in his introduction to *Writers at Work, Ninth Series*, said: "The tape recorder, together with a generally more polished and sophisticated approach on the part of the interviewers, has been an important factor in making these encounters livelier and more comprehensive, more densely textured and satisfying." He's referring to the *Paris Review* interviews, but this is true of author interviews in general.

In his introduction to *Writers at Work, First Series*, Malcolm Cowley considered the question of *why* such famous authors would take time away from their work to do an interview from which they had little to gain. He suspected that their agreement had more to do with friendship or the wish to help a struggling magazine than with any real desire to be interviewed. As the *Writers at Work* series gathered momentum, however, it became clear that authors were immersed in the writing process and eager to discuss their work. It was as if no one had ever thought to ask how it was done, and now, with someone sitting in front of them armed with a pencil and interesting questions, they were ready to talk.

The *Paris Review* allowed authors to contribute to their interviews by adding material, posing further questions, or editing their responses for purposes of clarification. The philosophy of the *Paris Review*, according to Plimpton, was that the writers being interviewed "were free to make what changes they wished since the intention of the editors was never to think of the interviews as inquisitions but rather as documentations of the authors-at-work."

Of the *Paris Review* interviews Plimpton says that there is such a wide range of opinion, style, habit, process, and taste that reading any collection may create more confusion than clarity in a young writer. But one hopes that through reading about the experiences of successful writers at work, new writers can find validation for their own efforts and the reading public can catch a glimpse of that all-too-mysterious figure: the writer.

## The Interview as an Evolving Form

The interview as a form has been present since Plato's *Dialogues* and even earlier, as a form of religious learning whereby a disciple asked questions of a wise man or teacher. The author interview, rather than offering a biographical *portrait* of a writer, offers a suggestive *glimpse*, and something more as well: a specificity of purpose, which gives it a narrative drive and structure. In general, a standard promotional author interview is structured around getting the author to talk about a recently published book. A more in-depth author interview, such as the *Paris Review* interviews and the interviews you learned to conduct in this book, has as its purpose the task of getting the author to talk about his work, the development of his craft, and the day-to-day practice of writing and living the life of the writer. In his introduction to *Writers at Work, Third Series,* Alfred Kazen says:

The classic interview, which Boswell and Eckermann practiced in order to write their respective books on Johnson and Goethe, is surely something else—a form of Wisdom literature. It seeks a Lesson From the Master (traditionally no smaller man is worth interviewing), and in it the interviewer plays the role of disciple. His job is to put the Master's views on life into book form . . . The classic interview with a Great Man probably had its origins in religious discipleship, and the purest example of it is still Plato's *Dialogues.* What the interviewer really asks is: How Are We To Live?

A profile [author interview], by contrast, is a sketch; what used to be called a "character"—a personality is quickly built up before our eyes. It is not an intellectual biography, such as a book on a single man seeks to become; it is a close-up, a startlingly informative glance—usually sympathetic, and even when it is not openly so, the coverage becomes a form of sympathy . . . It is not wisdom that we are trying to understand; it is exceptionality—in the case of a writer, his reputations as a writer, his hold on our imagination, means that for us he is like no one else. The interview becomes a way of getting the writer to document this exceptionality himself.

Throughout history, students have inquired of their mentors, whether religious, artistic, philosophical, or scientific, and this use of the interview to pursue serious lines of inquiry related to literature still holds critical value to aspiring writers and avid readers. Why not go straight to the source and ask the writer everything you want to know?

I would add to Kazen's description that the interview can have many more reasons or goals at the outset than divulging the nature of a writer's "exceptionality." In the case of the author interview, we are more interested in the details of how the writer continues to develop and execute his craft.

## The Future Is Now

The *Paris Review* interviews set the stage for the literary and other artistic interviews to follow. Literary magazines publishing fiction and poetry have since sprung up all over the world, offering their own versions of author interviews in ongoing attempts to grapple with all of the questions central to the life of the writer.

The first interviews I read were those compiled in the *Writers at Work* series, and those interviews have inspired and informed my own work. Anyone considering interviewing authors would be well served by reading and studying these collections. Several of them can be purchased directly from the *Paris Review*, at their website (www.parisreview.com), at bookstores, and especially, since most are out of print, in used bookstores and online used book sites.

Studying these classic interviews with some of the most famous writers in the world can help you come to an understanding about your own aesthetic preferences and intellectual curiosities; ultimately, it can help you decide the kind of interview you would like to conduct and publish. I hope the examples and exercises in this book help you to discover your own answers so that you can go into this work with your own voice and style.